Voices *of*
Southampton

Penny Legg

The History Press

For Thomas and Joe, a wedding present, with love.

First published 2011

The History Press
The Mill, Brimscombe Port
Stroud, Gloucestershire, GL5 2QG
www.thehistorypress.co.uk

British Library Cataloguing in Publication Data.
A catalogue record for this book is available from the British Library.

ISBN 978 0 7524 5819 9

Typesetting and origination by The History Press
Printed in Malta.

VOICES *of*

SOUTHAMPTON

CONTENTS

Penny Legg.

ACKNOWLEDGEMENTS

Where to start in a book that is comprised of the memories of the people who have grown up, lived, worked or travelled through the city? There are many to thank and I hope I have not forgotten any in the list below. If I have, I apologise and sincerely thank you – it was a pleasure to talk to you.

Joe Legg, my long-suffering husband, whose culinary skills get better each time I am immersed in a new writing project. Without his help and unfailing support, this book would not have been completed.

David Fakray and Jim Neal at the University of the Third Age in Southampton.

My creative writing class: Veronica Tippets, Jackie Early, Pat Hoy, Penny Cox, Jean Thompson and Douglas Brown.

The Writing Buddies: John Goodman, Tessa Warburg, Glen Jayson, Elizabeth Streatfield, James Marsh, Mo Foster.

Maureen Ashgar, Christine Bagg, Bill Benson, Jim Brown, Julie Green, Pat Collins, Sheila Cornwall, Carol Cunio, David Cox, Monica Cox, Douglas Easson and Ralph Easson of Easson's Coaches, John Easson, Julie Green, Margaret Griffin, John Gurney, Peggy Hale, Chris Hayles, Thomas Legg, Tessa Nelson-Humphries, Geoff Parker, Joan and Ron Shergold, John Sillence, Joan Smith, Pat Tarry, Joe Thorp, Eleanor van der Hoest, the late Moira van der Hoest, Binu Vijayakumari, Colin Warburg, the Hampshire Constabulary Historical Society.

I would particularly like to thank Eleanor van der Hoest, who came to see me one day to allow me to read her mother's life story. Moira van der Hoest died in 2008. She married her Dutch pen-friend, Niek. Before her death, her daughter recorded her talking about her life. Extracts of this memoir are published, in Moira's own words, for the first time in this volume, and I am very grateful to Eleanor for allowing this publication.

INTRODUCTION

This book is not meant to be a perfect history of the lives of Southampton people. Instead, it is a dip into the collective memory of those who have had, in one shape or form, a connection with the city. Memory is imperfect and subjective, so please bear this in mind as you turn the pages.

Researching this book has been a lot of fun. I have had the pleasure of meeting some super characters and heard a multitude of stories, told by an interesting and diverse range of people. These people have enthusiastically welcomed me into their homes, and kindly allowed me access to their photograph albums.

There were some groups I would have liked to include, but they either declined to be interviewed or could not decide how to be included and so missed my deadline. This is a shame as I think this snapshot of the city would have been the better for their participation, but I hope you enjoy the stories I have been able to bring you. They range from early pre-Second World War reminiscences to tales from the 1980s and the present.

Many books of this type have concentrated on the voices of its very oldest residents. Whilst there are undoubtedly more older voices in this book than young ones, I have also been interested to hear what the younger generation remember of their time in Southampton and so, some of the voices are distinctly dark-haired rather than grey.

I do hope you enjoy this book. My heartfelt thanks go to all those who made it possible. It was a real pleasure to meet so many interesting personalities. Southampton is a rich and diverse place and the voices that speak through the pages in this book reveal a unique, often funny, and never dull city.

Penny Legg, 2011

one

EARLY MEMORIES

New Arrivals

When my parents married, they rented two rooms in Victoria Road, Woolston (opposite the Thorneycroft Shipyard). Mother became pregnant, and the baby was due in May 1927. She was booked into the Clinic at New Road, Southampton, where the Southampton Institute now is. When labour started, a neighbour came with Mum. At night, the floating bridge ran, I believe, only on the hour. When the two women arrived at the floating bridge, the bridge went especially – 'woman in labour' was the cry. Arriving at the Clinic, they were told it was, 'full up,' given a bag of swabs, and told to go to the home of a nurse at Longhorn Road, Swaythling. The nurse was unkind to my mother; she told her not to scream and disturb the neighbours. Mum had a long labour with no pain relief and no company. So I was born on 9 May 1927, a healthy, dark-haired baby. I was always dressed in cream. Mum had made most of my clothes.

My father went across to Swift Road, the Keable grandparents' house, and threw some shingle up at the bedroom window. When Grandad opened the sash window, Dad told him, 'Leah's had a daughter.'

'Oh,' said Granddad, and shut the window. I was named Moira by my mother and Lucy by my father. Mum had heard the name Moira when she was employed by Dr Aldridge. The family had a son, Mr Norman, who had a young lady called Miss Moira. My Mum fell in love with the name, especially as pronounced by people who had had elocution lessons. My second name, Lucy, was Dad's mother's second name, although I have never liked it. I was christened at St Mark's, Woolston, my mother's two sisters being godmothers.

William Jesse Keable and Clara Jane (*née* Woolnough). William was a boilermaker with Thorneycrofts, moving to Southampton with the firm in about 1906. Moira remembers him as a harsh father who mellowed in old age. (Courtesy of Eleanor van der Hoest)

When my mother was expecting in 1929, the baby was born at home (after the previous bad experience). The midwife, Nurse Berry, was kind and Mum had every care. My brother was born on 25 July 1929, and again my Dad went across to the maternal grandparents' house and threw shingle up at the window. Grandad raised the sash window, and was told, 'Leah has a son.' The reply was 'Oh', and the window was slammed shut once again.

Moira van der Hoest

Water

We loved water and we had the Itchen just the other side of the railway, so that was fantastic. But we also looked for places in streams, so we could dam them. That was a great pastime. Then we would break the dam so we could watch the rush of water. We collected debris and waited until the water collected and then purposefully broke it. Quite why I was always standing in front of it when we did that I have no idea, but I got a very good view of the inrush of water as it hit me!

I never understood why we were not allowed to go out after having our hair washed. We had to wait for it to dry. If we went out with wet hair we would get all sorts of dreadful things, apparently.

James Marsh

Nursing Home

I was born in 1937 in the Totton nursing home. We were living in Nursling but my mother went to the nearest nursing home to us. There was nothing resembling a nursing home in Nursling! She took me back home when I was a few days old.

John Sillence

Edwin Jones

Edwin Jones was a big departmental store (bombed out in the war) – it is now Debenhams. Edwin Jones store had a large grocery department on the ground floor. In there was a huge machine, which cut up a wonderful, large mountain of butter into packaged half pounds. It clacked and ground its way through it all. It fascinated us children. We would stand and watch the machine, totally absorbed. Parents would leave their children, do the shopping, and come back to find the children had not moved.

Moira van der Hoest

How I Came to Love Mr Eyre

(Reproduced from the Southern Life website –www.southernlife.org.uk – by kind permission of Chris Hayles)

Long before the National Health Service and free treatment came into being, the local chemist was an extremely important person in the local communities; people used to visit them as many could not afford to pay for a doctor to treat them, unless it was an emergency. One of these chemists immediately springs to mind and that was old Mr Eyre, who was a dispensing chemist and had a shop near the end of Junction Road, near Batts Corner, Totton (next door but one to St Elmo, the nursing home where I was born).

He was a tiny man with almost white hair and always wore a white coat like a doctor. In fact I believe he did want to become a doctor but could not afford the training, so instead had opted for being a chemist, or in today's language, a pharmacist. Mind you, he was also an optician, did ear piercing and syringing, and would undertake a whole host of challenges. I remember having my mother drag me in there, screaming, to have him lance a boil on the back of my neck. Mr Eyre was renowned for his lack of bedside manner and just shouted at me and pushed me down into a chair! Some people used to say he was like a horse doctor and I believe he did dabble in veterinary practice! Though the shortages caused by the Second World War were extreme, his shop was always well stocked with practically anything to do with medicine and all that you could see was a short piece of counter to be served at, though often he would take customers out to the back of the shop to further discuss any treatment they might require. In fact, one particular day, my mother took me there and I had to stand in the shop while she went 'round the back' and discussed the fact that I had a rash on a delicate bit of my anatomy and could he prescribe something to ease the itching. He soon concocted some evil smelling ointment that I had to have rubbed on my backside twice a day, and which you could smell hours later when back at school. I found out later it contained Wintergreen oil! But most times you went there you had to queue up outside the shop and not a sound could be heard from the inside.

He often had his son, Timothy, help him in the shop, and he also had a daughter. In fact, I went to school with Tim, who, if I remember, was a tall, slim lad with a great big fuzz of fair curly hair.

Mr Eyre was one of the main players of the old Totton and I think everybody who was a child at that time lived in fear of him, but we have a lot to thank him for, even though he died an early death. He was a great loss to the town and will be remembered to this day.

Chris Hayles

Peggy

Our gran had a goat called Peggy. The goat used to wander around the filling station site here. There was no traffic on Spring Road in those days and there was a field on the opposite side, which was Gran's Field. There is a little river running down the back of Pinegrove Road and the goat used to run around and live over in the field. Our gran wanted to milk the goat. The problem was, it was not until she tried that she found out that it was a Billy goat!

The goat was the alarm – it would come and make a noise if a car pulled up on the forecourt. The original garage never had pumps. Petrol was sold in cans. During the war it got blitzed here when an incendiary came down. We did not have the fire brigade and

The Easson petrol station. Peggy the goat gave the alarm when a car came in. (Courtesy of Ralph and Douglas Easson)

so the chaps put it out. At the back of the garage there are a lot of subsidence problems because there is a big pit. The pit was filled in with sawdust, which came from the Super Marine factory in Woolston, because all the planes were wooden-framed. All the old scraps and sawdust were put in the big pit, to fill it. And of course, they all wandered why everything began to collapse - it was tonnes of wood!

Ralph and Douglas Easson

Goatee Beach

We used to go to Goatee Beach in Totton when we were kids. We wore woollen bathing costumes, which were unhelpful in the water. They became waterlogged. Goatee worried me a bit because of the posts with the black ball on the top indicating something for shipping. Sometimes the ball was up the top and sometimes it was down a bit. It might have been an indication of the tide. At the time, I was always worried about the ball. I was very young - we left Totton when I was seven. I am now eighty-three.

Joan Shergold

Outside Toilet

I remember visiting my grandparents' house in Cypress Avenue. When I was a small child, they had an outside toilet. You had to go out and round, it was all in the same building but you had to go outside, so it was always very cobwebby. As a child I was terrified of spiders and I would hold on and hold on and sometimes I couldn't go. We would sometimes have to spend a whole week there in the summer. I had to go to the toilet and I used to dread it. It was the most horrible thing. One time I got inside and there was a spider on the door and I had to pass it to get out. I was terrified!

Eleanor van der Hoest

Cowboys and Indians

We kids would come along and play cowboys and Indians, or pirates, and the chase was on, so off you went. First you went through the gardens, which had just been dug so nice and neatly and then we leapt over the fence, with the owner yelling after us,

'You ******* kids!' He had just laboured for hours and we had ruined it. We went over the fence, but, of course, you had to come back again, through the garden.

James Marsh

Working

Before mother left school, she had a job after school and some weekends looking after a baby. The child's parents owned a butcher's shop, the wife working in the little cash office. Before my father left school, he too had a job, delivering milk for Phipps of Netley Abbey. Later, he did the same work for Carters who had a farm at Peartree Green. At that time the workmen used to start work at 6 a.m. and come home for breakfast at 8 a.m. So when doing his milk rounds, he had to make sure the milk was delivered before 8 o'clock so there was fresh milk for the men's tea at breakfast. There were no fridges then, milk was delivered by copper measuring jugs into the customer's jug. In summer, the milk was always 'scolded' as soon as it was delivered to stop it going off. This meant simmering it very gently in a large shallow pan.

Moira van der Hoest

Shopping in Southampton

The thing I remembered, although I did not live in Southampton but over in the Waterside, in Holbury, was that Southampton was a Mecca. Most Saturdays were spent going over there and going shopping because there was nowhere at the Waterside to shop. Both my parents were from London and they were used to shops and things, so we were all dragged over to Southampton to go shopping. The shops were obviously different then – there was Mayes, and Edwin Jones. What was lovely shop at Christmas – in the window of Edwin Jones was a fairy story. We used to spend ages going all round the windows, they used to go right round the store. Each window had a separate bit of the story – Sleeping Beauty, for example - and we used to be absolutely captivated. It is Debenhams now.

Down there used to be butcher's shops, where the Lime Street car park is now. My parents used to go round there to get their meat and all the horrible things would be hanging outside, all covered in a cloth. The receptionist was in her glass coffin in the corner – they were behind a glass screen and they took the money, the butchers never handled the money. On the floor, there were inches of sawdust with blood and stuff on it. My dad was a really mean man and we had a car and he insisted on parking his car around the corner, so that they did not know we had a car. Sometimes they would look at him with all the four children, he was dressed shabbily, and think poor bloke, and he would get something knocked off his bill. He would whisper to us, 'Don't you tell them about the car around the corner.' So we used to park quite a way away and then go to the butcher's shop.

We used to come over to do our shopping for a long, long time because there was nothing in the Waterside. Mum used to go to Mac Fisheries, which was an early Sainsbury's I think, in the High Street. We always had to go there. We children used to hate being led around town. My parents, on occasion, would leave us at the playground in Hythe, which was a lovely playground, and go off to Southampton because we hated going into Southampton. I shudder to think about parents doing that now!

Jackie Early

The Dog and the Parrot

Gran had a marmoset and our Granddad had a pet fox. It got shot up on Dorking common in the end. Dad had three Alsatians and they used to know the timetable of the buses and when Dad used to arrive back; we did not have coaches in those days. One of the buses would turn up outside here and the dog would run out to greet him. The trouble was, he ran under the front wheel. Our dad killed it. The sad thing was that the dog and the family parrot were the best of friends. The parrot used to fly around of its own accord and stand underneath the outside tap. The dog would turn the tap on and wash the parrot! When the dog got killed, the parrot went to pieces. The parrot was given to the bird aviary as a second home.

Ralph and Douglas Easson

Art Deco

There used to be lots of fantastic art deco bus shelters in the city, but they have now disappeared.

Geoff Parker

On the Railway

My grandfather was on the railways. His patch was between Redbridge Station via Nursling Station, to Romsey. He had to make sure that nothing was wrong with the sleepers or the track. He walked up and down. It was steam trains. I said, 'I want to go on a steam train.' He said, 'You can't do that.' But he arranged with the driver to be at a certain place at a certain time but to slow down. So I got on the bend there and the train slowed right down and I put a foot on the footplate and got carried around the bend and then I got off again. I was in junior school. Nursling station closed in 1957. You can go through Nursling station still. It is on the main Salisbury line.

John Sillence

Steam Trains

I remember the last steam train leaving Southampton Central Station. I was down there with my father, he took us down there and we watched the last one leave. I was eleven. The smoke is my biggest memory. They always pulled the whistle and let the smoke off under the bridge. So he would go under the bridge, the driver pulled the whistle and all the smoke came up as he went through. We were on the footbridge, which is still there. I got enveloped in the steam!

Pat Collins

The attraction of the steam train was the steam. For ten seconds you seemed like you were invisible and then your eyes were stinging and burning.

Geoff Parker

Egg and Coal Dust

My mother was a make-do cook. She used to make these great big suet puddings because they filled us up – anything that filled us up was fine. Egg and chips was always on a Saturday. Every other Saturday we had the added ingredient of coal dust, because the cupboard in the corner of the room should have been a larder but my mother had it as a coalhouse. We were always sitting around the table when the coal man came with a hundredweight of coal on his back. He walked round the table, opened the

Steam engines are still popular, as seen by the crowds here at the Eastleigh 100 years celebration in 2009. (Author's collection)

door and heaved the coal into the larder. Of course, a great plume of coal dust came up and no matter how much we covered our plates, it still settled on our egg and chips!

James Marsh

Saturday Morning Pictures

We walked into Shirley on Saturdays. The Regent cinema was there. The Regent gave us the children's morning, so we went in there. It was opposite Sainsbury's in the precinct. We had a main film – usually a cartoon or a cowboy with Roy Rogers – and some adverts of a small nature, and we had a packet of crisps and a drink. By the time we left, the staff were at their wits end! I did that every Saturday morning for about four years when I was growing up. It cost pence – 10d or less. All the children went there from all the villages around and they all shouted at the screen. They all asked their parents for money for a bag of chips for on the way back. I don't think there is as much of that now. The cinemas are only in Southampton. The Regent is gone now.

John Sillence

Broadway Cinema

During the period 1944 to 1949 I would go with my twin sister Maureen to the Broadway cinema in Portswood, which is now a bingo hall, to Saturday morning pictures for kids. We would see things like *Old Mother Riley*, Roy Rogers' cowboy films and cartoons. It was very noisy, with unsupervised children all shouting their heads off. It cost 6d in old money to get in.

David Cox

New Year

Mother-in-law lived in Shakespeare Road, Portswood, and on New Year's Eve during the fifties we would see the New Year in. The ships' sirens would go off in the docks and we would bang dustbin lids together.

Monica Cox

The Southampton Docks. (Courtesy of Julie Green.)

The Crypt

When I was about eight years old, about 1947 or so, on the corner of East Street, Southampton, there was an old church that had been bombed out during the Second World War. We used to go and play in it. We would open the squeaking iron gate that led to the crypt and go down and play there in the dark.

David Cox

Pigs

There was always a separate container for food waste at school, for the pigs!

Elizabeth Streatfield

The Vicar

The Vicar ran the village. I remember that the kids used to kick a ball about and mine went through a greenhouse owned by just about the most severe woman in Nursling. She came roaring out but the Vicar said, 'Your aim is awful.' He put a ball through the next pane! She came out to say, 'Here, you!' but ended up saying, 'Hello Vicar, how are you?'

John Sillence

A Promise Remembered

In 1943, my mother was in the Ack Ack in the New Forest, shooting down the enemy planes. She fell in love with the area and I remember, as a small boy, her dearest wish was to retire to Southampton. It was a bit alien to my father, being a Scotsman. I think his idea was to go to Edinburgh. Her name was Amelia, or Millie for short. Monday to Friday she spelt it with an 'ie' and at the weekend it was Milly! She was a bit of a character. She retired as a copy typist in 1985, within months of my father retiring from the London Underground, where he was a ticket clerk. She won the argument and they went to Southampton. They looked at various properties and they found one on Lewis Silkin Way in Lordshill. They lived there from 1985 until my mother passed on in 1995. My father Ronald, who was known as Jock to the locals, died in 2008.

John Easson

Ronald 'Jock' Easson with his wife Amelia (Millie, centre) and Emily, a relative, at their dream retirement home in Southampton. (Courtesy of John Easson)

The Bakers

When I was about ten or twelve years old and the family lived in Portswood, behind Lowman's bakers, which was in Portswood Road, we used to go and get freshly baked, hot bread at 10 p.m. on a Sunday night. We should have been in bed ready for school the next day really, but it didn't seem to worry Mum.

Maureen Ashgar (née Cox)

The Grand Theatre

I remember getting off a bus at the Hants and Dorset bus station on Windsor Terrace in the early 1950s, and walking past the Grand Theatre on the corner. Mum would hurry past there, but I could see all the pictures of scantily-clad ladies who looked very naughty!

Penny Cox

Real Bears!

I remember being taken in the 1950s, by my sister Dolly, to the Grand Theatre on the corner of Civic Centre Road and Windsor Terrace, to see *Goldilocks and the Three Bears*, with three live bears!

Maureen Ashgar (née Cox)

Flying

The railway was a grass section and then a bank with the line on the top. There were hoardings – 'No rubbish to be thrown on railway property, signed …' No one ever took any notice of these, so all the way along there were pots and pans, old bikes, prams; anything we didn't want, over to the railway it went. That is where we kids, I was six or seven at the time, went looking for what we needed. We made our own bikes, we used pram wheels for trolleys and most of it came from there. If we could not find it elsewhere, it was go look for it on the railway. We found saddles and we found wheels and frames but no pedals, tyres or brakes, so it was two boys, one each side, running like mad and who let go and it clattered along the pavement. We got told off about the noise. We loved it, legs flying as there were no pedals and we were just hanging on trying to steer, to see how far it could go.

You went down the first slope and then you had to lean to the right, we had no tyres, so you had to haul the bike round and then it went down the smaller, very steep slope and then you had the long stretch. So it was push off and you were off, away. My friend Pat pushed off, down he went, flying like mad, wonderful! We were waiting for him to take the turn and we are still waiting! He didn't turn and there was a trench and his bike hit that and he was airborne – Evel Knievel would have been very proud of him – and he was going into the Wheeler's back garden. Mrs Wheeler did the gardening and the runner beans were growing to her satisfaction and then this apparition comes over her back fence – Pat had crashed, taking the runner beans with him. So, of course, he got off his bike and ran. But, being a community, Mrs Wheeler went to see his mother and his mother was waiting for him when he came home. He was limping a bit for a few days and sitting down very gingerly.

James Marsh

The Monkeys

The kids, for a special treat, used to go for a ride with their pocket money but the monkeys used to take advantage – on the very old buses they used to try and jump up on the back step, for a free lift. They stopped them doing that because my granddad ran a cable from the magneto to the brass handles and if a kid got on they got a shock and they soon jumped off! You would be done by the health and safety now!

Ralph and Douglas Easson

Ruby Road

My maternal grandfather, William Lucas, was in horticulture of some sort, I believe. He had a strawberry field just off Middle Road and he bought a plot of land in Lodge Road, which is now Ruby Road, and he had a house built there in 1885. Round the back was a stable, which was actually still there when I was a youngster. There was a shed with a great big copper for the clothes and a well. My father, Frederick, bought the house off of him when he and mum, Louisa (Cissy) got married. My mother was born in the house and so was I.

Ron Shergold

William Lucas with the house he had built in 1885. (Courtesy of Ron Shergold)

Hiding a Shilling

I went regularly to the fantastic art deco open-air Lido. It was a fabulous place. It was a great feeling in the open air and it was always busy in the summer. It's about where Toys R Us is now. I went with the kids I went to school with. We used to get undressed in the cubicles and we had to hide our money in our socks or people would go in and take it. A shilling was quite a lot of money to me.

Geoff Parker

two

TEENAGE YEARS

Fifteen Going on Twelve

I was a skinny, very, very young-looking kid. So at fifteen I looked like somebody's twelve-year-old brother, which is why I got nowhere with girls! My great friend was Edward Wheeler and we went on an outing. We ended up at a dance and there were girls there.

'Can I have this dance?'

'NO!'

The girl danced with Edward. I was furious – I was much better than him! *Why is she dancing with him,* I thought. Perhaps because he looked his age and I didn't. I had no chance!

James Marsh

The Carnival

In the days when Southampton had a town carnival and people were invited to join a procession, which happened every so often, I came up with the idea that I would like to enter it. I didn't know what to do, so I decided to make myself a chicken. In the photograph, they are my legs going along inside the chicken! My friend Peter Bassil is beside me. His father kept the chemist at the top of Bedford Place. Bassil the Chemist is still there. We were about fourteen or fifteen. I built this thing out of wire and bits of wood and made it like a cockerel and then I processed up and down. It was pretty heavy after walking two or three miles. We started outside the town walls and walked up past Bargate, right to the top to Southampton Common.

Douglas Brown

Top Rank

The Top Rank Suite was a new concept for Southampton as it was a dance hall, nightclub and disco, all under one roof. It opened in the mid-1960s and was demolished in the late 1980s. The annual Southampton Press Ball was held there, featuring top cabaret names of the day, such as Roy Castle and Jimmy Tarbuck.

As teenagers, we used to walk right down from Town Quay after coming off the Hythe Ferry, right up to Top Rank, which used to be in Banister Road, which is a long way! We used to come up there with our smart shoes on and no money for the bus! We just didn't think about the long way and could not afford to get a bus.

I remember as teenagers it had quite a strict dress code and my boyfriend Brian – now my husband – had long hair, which was tucked into his collar and they would not let him in. So, we went round to a friend's house nearby to cut the back of his hair with the bacon scissors. It was all crooked. We rushed back but we were too late; it was full, we could not get in. He had a perm later.

Jackie Early

Douglas Brown in his chicken outfit for Southampton Carnival. (Courtesy of Douglas Brown)

Brian Early with his 'long hair'. The motorcycle belonged to a friend. (Courtesy of Jackie Early)

I tried to smoke my first cigarette at Top Rank. I was eighteen in 1964. We always felt very grown up, sophisticated and mature there. We would sit there with our glasses of Bacardi, which was fashionable then. I ended up in a cloud of smoke. I didn't get the idea of inhaling. So smoking didn't catch on with me!

Elizabeth Streatfield

In the 1960s we used to go to Top Rank, where the ice rink used to be. Top Rank was 8s 6d, the most expensive in Southampton. We used to go to the Guildhall, that was 5s. We used to really love the pier. It was 5s too. We would come over on the Hythe ferry. We would go to Hythe and come over, go into the pier and there was one of these big silver balls that went round and cast light on you. Outside, people were doing their courting on their seats. You would get all hot in there and then you would go outside and have a kiss and a cuddle outside on the seats and then you would get on the horrible Hythe ferry, which was terribly smelly. There were seats downstairs where the engine was or you could sit on the deck outside on the Hythe ferry, but it got very cold in the middle. It was not very nice.

The Hythe Ferry. (Courtesy of Julie Green)

At the pier we did not dress up much. There was a strict dress code for these places – Top Rank was always smart, Guildhall was fairly smart but at the pier you dressed down, so we only ever wore a skirt and a blouse or something like that. It was thought to be common; my parents didn't like me going to the pier. One of the places that was very 'in' in the High Street was the Casbah. It was a coffee bar, but everyone wanted to go and hang out in the Casbah. I couldn't afford the 5s bus fare to come over and hang about there.

Jackie Early

I met my husband at Top Rank. I was there with my friend. He asked me to dance. My first impression was, *Ooh, he's nice looking, he's polite, he's smartly dressed.* He had nice dark hair and blue eyes. He was not a good dancer. He told me afterwards he didn't really like dancing. He had a car. That impressed me; it was a Triumph Mayflower.

Elizabeth Streatfield

The Pier

The pier was a bit rougher and you sat outside for a bit of … [dissolves laughing and blushing].

Jackie Early

The New Pier. (Courtesy of Julie Green)

My sister used to tell my dad that she was at the Guildhall when she was at the pier!

Veronica Tippetts

The Guildhall

We went to the Guildhall on a Wednesday night. It was ballroom dancing there but older people went – older men! It was just a change to go ballroom dancing rather than jiving or jitter bugging. I went with a friend.

Elizabeth Streatfield

Jazz and Romance

The jazz club where the Hobbit is now was called the Yellow Dog Jazz Club. It was down in the basement and it used to be all 'black and trad' jazz. We used to go stomping there. Stomping is just putting your foot down very flat and hard on the floor with a kind of skipping sort of movement. In the basement it was very dark, with water dripping off the walls. It was packed, crammed tight with people. I was seventeen and I kind of thought I was a bit of a beatnik. I wasn't really but that's what I thought I was!

I met my husband in the Yellow Dog Jazz Club. It was all dark and dingy and I was being a teenager. I thought I knocked his beer over. I said, 'I'm terribly sorry, I think I've knocked your beer over.' And he said, 'I should jolly well hope not!' He certainly charmed the birds out of the trees! I actually fancied his friend! He was twenty-three and he took me home, all the way to Eastleigh, afterwards – after saying, 'I only live over the road.'

He came to the bus stop with me and actually got on the bus and then he had to go all the way out to Eastleigh and then come all the way back to Portswood.

We got married three years later and will have been married forty-six years in September 2011.

Penny Cox

Getting Together

I was still at school when I started to go out with Brian. We both went to St Patrick's Church. He was an altar boy, so I had spotted him. I went to the girls' grammar school and he used to go to King Edward's. We had to change buses and the bus stops were next to each other – he would get on that one and I'd get on the other. He would nod to me. Then I went to the Catholic Youth Club in Bitterne. I was very scared, all on my own. I rode my bike up there, walked in and he was the first person I saw. I went out with another boy for a year, and then Brian, and I started being friendlier. He came to my sixteenth birthday party. It was such a long time ago.

Carol Cunio, Mayor of Southampton, 2010/2011

Progress

It took a month to get my arm around a girl. It took two weeks to get to the back row of the cinema. It took ages and then finally I got that far and the first time I got my arm round her and I leant my head towards her, she said, 'Mind my hair, I've just had it done!' It was a bit of a dampener. All that work, all that patience and she is more worried about her hairdo! I was sixteen. So I went to sea instead!

James Marsh

Boyfriends

My parents were not very keen on any of my boyfriends. They thought I was going to get pregnant! They really did. Nothing was further from my mind! I was too scared. Mum said, 'He's a Catholic, you'll have babies every year.' We were Catholic, too. That is what she was worried about. When we were married, I had six babies.

Carol Cunio, Mayor of Southampton, 2010/2011

Trans-Atlantic Flirting

I went cabin class, in the middle between first class and tourist class, on the *Queen Mary* and also on *Queen Elizabeth*. They would pass each other mid Atlantic. I also sailed on the SS *America* and the SS *France*. That was the way people travelled in those days. My father was in New York. It was incredibly enjoyable and you had five days' holiday. I just went down to the docks and got on the boat. It was very convenient! There weren't any of the cargo boats. I just remember the liners.

The SS *America* was my first liner. I was nineteen. I was in a cabin with three other women and a couple of them were quite experienced travellers. They told me how to go on. I don't get seasick, so that was another plus. It did get choppy and I remember having the dining room almost to myself. I played deck quoits while the boat was rising and falling. It was great fun! There was flirting, too, and it was all quite safe, as I was with these other women, so I could flirt. I flirted with young men who happened to be on the trip. I don't know why they were on the trip. I didn't see any of them ever again! I remember playing chess. There was a serious young man who liked playing chess. I had not seen my father for a very long time because there was a war in between and I remember playing chess with this young man and taking no notice of the fact that the boat had docked and probably my father was coming up to see me. One is so horrible as a young person!

Tessa Warburg

Glamorous Photos

My sister is seven years my senior. I asked her where she got the gown from in the photograph and she explained to me. So I thought, *Blow! I am going to do that if my big sister can do it.* I went

Veronica Tippetts' (*née* Peet) sister, Betty. The 'gown' was a piece of blackout material. (Courtesy of Veronica Tippetts)

Veronica Tippetts (*née* Peet) keeping up with her big sister. (Courtesy of Veronica Tippetts)

along to Donald Herbert, the photographer in Commercial Road at Chandler's Studio. It was a bit embarrassing, actually, having to take off my top with a man there, so he just said, 'Get behind there.' So I went behind a screen and that was fine. But actually, what I noticed was that he had a look at me. My breasts were a little bit tiny, compared with others, you know, but he looked and he said, 'You have lovely breasts, would you like to come and pose?' I said. 'No, I couldn't go in for that.' He was a photographer, and there was no question of anything but that he was looking at my body as a photographer would. He gave me a bit of blackout material. I came out from behind the screen with the material draped around me and the photo was taken. I was about seventeen. It is a sophisticated pose, because my sister had had hers taken and so what I did was copy my sister.

Veronica Tippetts

The Grand Theatre

We had never seen naked girls. The nearest we got was when they went swimming and then we only got to see their knickers. It was all a big thrill because it was the best we could do at fourteen. We started going to the Grand Theatre and sitting up in the gods and we were told a nude review was coming. And when we heard what this was – naked ladies would be on the stage – we got our tickets then and there! We told everyone that we were going to see naked ladies on the stage and they would have *nothing* on at all! We were in our seats and then the curtains opened. There were these pillars and we thought, where are the ladies? 'They are behind the pillars,' we were told. 'They have nothing on, but they are not allowed to move and be seen.' I think we saw a knee sticking out and the odd toe. That was it! It was a swizzle! The place was packed and they started to boo. We were right in the front too, terrific seats! It was some time before I actually saw a naked lady.

James Marsh

The Floating Bridge

I was about sixteen years old. It must have been in the school summer holidays because it was before I went to work. It happened in the rush hour and if I had been working, I would not have been messing about in a boat on the river, I would have been on the floating bridge. It must have been about July or August when I was sixteen. I was born in June 1952. I had a boyfriend, who later became my first

The *Queen Elizabeth* in Ocean Dock. (Courtesy of Douglas Brown)

husband. His name was Dennis. His family lived in Itchen, overlooking the floating bridge. This all happened before they started constructing the new bridge. He had a little dinghy boat with an outboard engine and a day cabin on it. He was absolutely mad about fishing. He was always asking me to go fishing with him. I tried it out but I was not very interested. So then one day, he said, 'Well, why don't you come out in the boat with me and we'll try fishing from the boat, you might like that better, it's easier.' He must have had a day off work and we went out in this little boat with the outboard engine and I was bored to tears!

We went down Southampton Water and we did some fishing and then we were coming back at about five o'clock. You had to wait for the floating bridges to pass if you were in a small craft. They had a signalling system – they had a big black ball that was hoisted on a pole and when the big black ball was up, the floating bridge was starting to cross. They did it, I think, to signal to each other because they crossed in unison, the two bridges, and they passed in the middle of the river. That is how they timed it when they were setting off. They also timed it so that they would get to the other side in time for all the buses to pick passengers up and the bus drivers timed it so that they pulled away as everyone was streaming off the floating bridge and racing up the ramp to try to catch the bus. You would see all the empty buses driving off.

On this particular day we were going along and we waited and the bridges had crossed and we were set to go through the middle while they were loading up with dockers. The one from Woolston was on our right and that bridge was pretty near empty. It was the bridge on the left that was absolutely packed because all the dockers were coming home. We ran out of two-stroke, the fuel the engine used. We actually ran out right in the path between the two floating bridges; it just died! So we just sort of sat there and we saw the black balls go up – of course, the bridges wanted to cross. I started to panic, what should we do? Dennis said, 'Well, we will just have to row! Grab an oar and start rowing'. So, I was rowing and we were actually just going round and around in a circle because I can't row. We could hear car horns blaring from off the floating bridge – they wanted us to get out of the way; the passengers wanted to go home. In the end, I think they thought we were just messing about. But we just could not get out of the way! The bridge from the Woolston side did not cross but the one from the town side did, because they were impatient. They stopped in the middle by where we were and the flow of the tide washed us up on to the platform. Dennis jumped out onto the platform. I sat there in that boat, the *Blue Peter*, and it

A charming 1950s study of the floating bridge, painted by John Chipp. (Courtesy of Christine Bagg)

was one of the most embarrassing experiences in my life! All these dockers hanging over the gate – they were not complimentary! They told us to get out of the way. You could see all their bicycles, all lined up. Eventually, Dennis did push the little boat out and he had to row both oars himself. Finally, we got out of the way. I didn't go out in the boat again after that.

Actually, my mum felt sorry for Dennis because I would not go out in the boat. He came around one evening and was saying that I should give it another chance and mum said to him, 'Well, I'll come out with you!' He was a nice young man, so what could he say. So he actually went out with my mum in his boat, which was lovely of him. On the way back, he started scrabbling around in the boat and I remember her describing it to me – 'What's happened, what's happened?' He said, 'Don't worry, the bung's come out!' He was trying to put the bung back in the bottom of the boat. I don't know if he did that deliberately to discourage her. To take the girlfriend out is one thing, to take the girlfriend's mother out, I don't know.

Christine Bagg

three

EDUCATING SOUTHAMPTON

Ludlow Road School

Both my parents' families (Mortimers and Keables) attended Ludlow Road School, Woolston, Southampton. My mother and father always referred to the school as 'Ludlow College', because of its high educational standard.

My mother was a good student, and, at age eleven, was informed by her teacher that she had been chosen to sit the scholarship examination (later called the Eleven Plus) to enable her to go to grammar school. Mother went home in the lunch break quite happy and told her father, who instantly replied, 'Oh no you're not, my girl. It's domestic service for you, as soon as you're old enough. Put your feet under someone else's table.'

Moira van der Hoest

Mini Skirts

My mother was a dressmaker, and made all our wedding dresses. My youngest sister wanted her dress above the knee but my mother wouldn't allow it and it had to be just below the knee. I used to teach in school. I was working with teenage girls and I told them that fashion goes round and round. Mini skirts were in in 1924!

Joan Shergold

Taken in the garden of the family home in Bitterne Road in 1923, the bride and groom are Beatrice Annie Louise Miller (*née* Laverty) and Frederick Miller. The bride was a dressmaker and made her own, and all her sisters', wedding gowns. (Courtesy of their daughter, Joan Shergold)

Nursling Church of England School

I went to school in 1942, in the middle of the war – Nursling Church of England School and there was Rownhams C of E school. We had to trudge up there to school every morning and it was quite religious. You had to have a prayer at the gate before you got in and that was the way we were brought up. I think there was a lot of benefit in that because when we got to eleven years old and they introduced the Eleven Plus exam, we had about 98 per cent success through keeping to traditional methods. The headmistress was so good in the end that when they built Rownhams they named a close after her – Adcock Close, for her services to teaching.

John Sillence

Merry Oak School

In our first term at Merry Oak, the one thing that I remember well is being instructed to write between the lines. Thick strokes down and thin strokes up. I remember Mr Permain used to come into the lesson whenever we had composition or some kind of writing exercise. He would walk up and down the aisles, jingling his keys or money in his pocket. This would stop immediately he spotted a poor soul not doing her thin strokes up, and thick strokes down. We were all in awe of him. Somehow, we managed this new exercise. Later, however, came a bigger surprise, when we were instructed to write on plain paper, and in straight lines!

Moira van der Hoest

Taunton School

I was at Taunton School, in Highfield, not the Tauntons College of today. The Latin master, Art Colborne – we called him Cod – said, 'There is one way of teaching a boy Latin – with his *Kennedy's Latin Primer* and 18 inches of thin cane.' You learn Latin very rapidly that way. Every year he ran a camp and all the boys on

The majestic lines of Taunton School. (Courtesy of Douglas Brown)

it had kit inspections. Iron discipline was kept. If anyone went into the tents after lights out, Cod would come down with a strap and belt people's bottoms. This was how education was. None of us resented it. It was a great school with fantastic teaching staff. Dr H.M. King, the Speaker of the House of Commons, was the English master at the school and he taught me English. Mr Speaker taught Dougy Brown!

Douglas Brown

Methodists

We went to the Methodist Church Sunday School in Redbridge Lane because they gave us lemonade for refreshments. So we became Methodists! That was pulled down. They grassed the site and now it is part of the recreation ground in Southampton. I think they call it Ten Acres.

John Sillence

Middle Road Infants' School

One time, I gave a talk to a class about the school when I was a pupil there. One boy asked me if we had slates and chalk. I said, 'No, pencils and books.' The next question went the other way – did we have computers? Ah well, times change.

Moira van der Hoest

Coal Fires and Violins

When I got to school, my first job was to clean out the coal fires. The teachers lit them. In those days the village people just had to help out and the children did too. We had to do that before we started lessons.

Before we had our lesson Mrs Slow, our teacher, had to get her violin out and do a hymn because we were a Church of England school. We all sang along.

John Sillence

The Gregg School

I was at the Gregg School between 1966 and 1971. The headteacher in my first year was an ex-army man who was very strict and most people were very frightened of him. He retired after my first year. Then we had Rory Birch, who was the history teacher at the school and then got the headship. He only lasted about four years and as I left, Roger Hart took over. He only retired in 2010. We had a French teacher who was Italian and when she got frustrated she would shout at us in Italian. She was a bit scary – one of those volatile Italians. She was sweet one moment and then would erupt. We had a French student, quite an attractive young lady, who would ride her bike with a very short skirt on. All the elder boy pupils would be lining up to watch her ride in and get off, to see her knickers, and the male teachers would line up inside, looking out of the window.

The PE teacher was a Mrs Winstone or Brimstone, one of these elderly, prim and proper Joyce Grenfell types, all jolly hockey sticks. 'Girls, girls,' she'd say, 'come this way.' There wasn't a playing field at the school. In order to do PE, which was all Wednesday afternoons, we would go across to the common and play rounders

Margaret Griffin, in brand new school uniform, off to join the Gregg School. (Courtesy of Margaret Griffin)

and do athletics. It was also her job to give us the basic sex education, as was in those days. We didn't have sex education then, it was not even thought of. You didn't even talk about reproduction. She would do the hygiene aspect of it and she would talk about washing one's hair and keeping one's face and nails and hands clean – she would go down the body and stop at the waist. It was only girls, but she would not talk about anything to do with being female or reproduction. We were all thinking, *well, perhaps she will wait until we are all in the fifth year*. No. Never. I think she was so embarrassed that she just could not go there. She had a bright pink hat and a Joyce Grenfell dress and summer and winter that hat was on. She was a character.

Major Treadwell taught maths and physics. He was ex-army and on the point of retirement. He was very much the sergeant major type of personality. He would not take any fuss or nonsense whatsoever, but he had no idea how to teach. He knew his subject but he had no idea how to put it across. He spent most of his time writing on the board while we played havoc in the background. He would turn around and glare at us and then carry on at the blackboard.

Clive Herring taught geography. He came to us as a brand new teacher in my second year. He was a nice guy but every other word he said was, 'right'. He would finish a sentence by saying, 'such and such and such and such, right?' Sometimes, we just sat there and counted how many times he said 'right' on a five bar gate. We had a new kid start in the middle of the term. He didn't know what the names of the teachers were and we kidded him that Clive Herring's name was Mr Kipper. He didn't know any different. So when it was time to put his hand up to answer a question, he said, 'Mr Kipper.' We started to giggle. Clive Herring didn't know whether to laugh, or shout at this lad.

Margaret Griffin

Memories from School

From 1998 to 2001, I attended the Gregg School after spending three years in Belgium with my parents. For some reason or another, I have trouble remembering much of my time spent there, however, just a few things have stuck in my mind.

I was selected to attend the Mayor Making ceremony at the City Hall in Southampton. The school required two pupils to attend the ceremony as their representatives and this year it was my turn, as I was the senior prefect (essentially the deputy to the deputy head boy). My female counter-part, Suzy, and I duly accepted the offer and we were packed off in a taxi to Southampton City Centre. I remember expecting a teacher to accompany us; however it turned out to be just Suzy and myself. Having an afternoon off school plus an unaccompanied taxi ride to and from the city turned out to be far more exciting than the ceremony itself – neither Suzy nor I could remember much about the event once we returned to school. I can remember seeing, amongst the audience of attending dignitaries and visitors, an officer from one of the nearby military bases who had a look of total boredom on his face – probably much like myself! Still, at the age of sixteen anything was better than an afternoon at school.

My other memory is of our school play one year. Our headmaster, Mr Hart, had chosen *Oklahoma*, which was great for me as I had secretly wished to be a cowboy (maybe I watched too many John Wayne movies when I was younger!). My wish was soon granted as I was cast as a cowboy and issued with a rifle, which I was to carry in some of my scenes. However, I soon decided that I should definitely carry it as much as possible, which ended up being every scene I was in – even when I was only in the chorus and standing in the background. On the final night, Mr Hart asked me why I carried the gun all the time, so instead of telling him, I decided to show him. On one side of the butt stick I had a sheet of paper, which had a load of my lines - all the ones I had trouble remembering! Thankfully, I rarely needed my 'cheat sheet' but I ended up spending an extraordinary amount of time trying to make sure that the audience couldn't see that sheet of paper!

Thomas Legg

The Gondoliers

I was at Taunton's School from the age of fourteen to the age of eighteen. I was about sixteen when I was in the opera *The Gondoliers*. I was a courtier in the first part of the play. Taunton's School was a boys' school. Gregory Hiscock is in the blond wig and Gordon Harper is in the dark one. Later in the opera, you have to become a gondolier and we sang the chorus. The chap with the moustache is Micheal Brown. We were the two Browns. He was the son of the German master at Taunton's School and he went off and got ordained and became a Bush Brother in Australia. I had ideas about being ordained but ended up being a schoolteacher, which I am glad I did. My voice was still a treble then.

Douglas Brown

Douglas Brown and friends from
Taunton School in *The Gondoliers*.
(Courtesy of Douglas Brown)

The two Browns in *The Gondoliers*.
(Courtesy of Douglas Brown)

Student Life

I first came to Southampton in 1947 as an undergraduate, on a County Major Scholarship, to read mathematics in what was then University College, Southampton, where we took external London degrees. I went to a convent school and then to grammar school in Oxted, Surrey, for 'A' levels and there was a girl there who had gone to Southampton from the school and said how nice it was, and how much she had enjoyed it, so I applied to a number of places and I got into London but it was a women's college and I thought, *I don't really want to go into a women's college. I want to meet some men*! I never regretted it. I enjoyed Southampton. I really liked it.

It was very difficult to get into college in those days because priority was given to the ex-servicemen, so most of my male fellow students were just that. The maths department was nice and small. There were only ten students. There was one other woman. Because I had not done any applied maths, going from the convent I had not done any science, and pure maths I found easier to work out for myself, but the applied maths was much more difficult. So the county paid for me to take 'A' level applied maths. That was a class of forty men and me at the university. A lot of the ex-servicemen had to do that, too. This was primarily an engineering college. It was quite funny with them. Being ex-servicemen they were much more inclined to do what they wanted rather than what the lecturer wanted. He didn't like them coming in late. So, one day, he decided to lock the door, so there I was locked in with all these men, which I thought was quite unsuitable!

They were quite shy but I loved to go to dances and I loved going by myself, because I wanted to meet various people. I didn't want to just meet one boy and then not know anything about men, really. So they used to dance with me, because I was the only girl they knew! It was great fun and very useful indeed.

I lived in Highfield Hall for four years and didn't have to go into digs because my mother – we were refugees from Hitler in 1938 – had gone back to Austria in 1947 and because my father (my parents were divorced) lived in New York. I often sailed between Southampton and New York, once on the first *Queen Elizabeth* and also on the *Queen Mary*.

I was what they called an overseas student and I was entitled to live in halls all the time, which was very nice. I also thoroughly enjoyed it. It was all women. You were allowed visitors at certain times of the day, fixed hours, and, of course, when you went out in the evening you had to sign out and sign in again and had to be in by 10 o'clock; I actually I also liked this because it meant that if you didn't

The Port of Southampton in all her glory. (Courtesy of Julie Green.)

particularly want to go on seeing someone you could escape! All the girls used that. People thought it was oppressive – it wasn't. It was quite useful.

Tessa Warburg

Mature Student

My husband got a place as a student on a chemistry degree course at Southampton University. We were living in Bournemouth. We thought we would come to Southampton for three years and then go back to Bournemouth and here I am, forty years later! He was a mature student. We got a decent grant. I was the bread winner. I was lucky, I got promoted in the Civil Service in Bournemouth, I got expenses to move to Southampton and in 1970 Southampton City Council was very forward thinking and they did mortgages. They actually gave mortgages to women! It was quite unheard of. So, I have always been grateful to Southampton because it got us on the housing ladder. We bought half a house round the corner from the university – a self-contained flat in Welbeck Avenue – and friends laughed at us. 'You'll never be able to sell it.' We actually did OK. We had students living in our second bedroom for a while and we managed quite well.

We saw all the lads walking past Welbeck Avenue, with their hair down to their waist and the old Sergeant Pepper moustaches, and that is how Alan Whitehead looked – he was President of the Southampton Students' Union and he had beautiful long black hair and moustache.

It was a nice time. In those days around the university it was mainly family houses. When we had the second child on the way we moved to a semi-detached round the back of the university and it was all young couples doing places up where old people had died. There were hardly any cars. It is student land now.

Glen Jayson

Cornish Pasties

After I had the kids, I went to university in Southampton. Brian took Stephen up to Manchester because he was starting his degree. We had taken Celia, our daughter, up to the police cadets at Bishops Waltham. So, on one day the two of them left home and then, the next morning, I started my degree. All change! I knew I had one lecture that didn't finish until five on a Thursday and there were six of us at home. I knew it was a ten-week term, so I made sixty Cornish pasties, big ones, which my kids love. They were in the freezer so on a Thursday morning I would get these out, put them in the oven on a timer and when we came home, they were ready. I did not have to do it again because next term the lectures changed. The kids always remembered that though, they loved Thursdays!

Carol Cunio, Mayor Southampton 2010/2011

Southampton City College

I had been at boarding school and was now out in the big wide world, doing a secretarial course at the City College. The guy who was the principal at the college was there and he addressed us all, as it was the beginning of the year.

'I was a Navvy!' he said. That was the principal of the college – you would not get that today. The working class could make their way through education then.

Veronica Tippetts

Halls

I was a student at Southampton University in 1975. I studied biochemistry and physiology. It seemed to be quite a modern university. I was working in Boldrewood, the medical block, and it was quite open and friendly.

The first year I was up at Glen Eyre hall. That was shared between twenty people and we had one kitchen and we used to take it in turns occasionally to cook the Sunday meal. I had done things like that before – we used to take it in turns as children to cook on Sunday. Some people were better at it than others!

Sometimes we would have long discussions late into the night – usually with lawyers – taking opposing views, which was quite fun.

Colin Warburg

The Frog and Frigate

We used to do pub-crawls down Portswood, close to Halls. We would go from Stoneham into town, crossing roads and going into various pubs as we went through. Then, often we would end up at the Frog and Frigate, in Canute Road. I don't know if that is still open. We would dance on the tables – it was a spit and sawdust pub. Those were fun times. We would go as a group – half a dozen or ten of us.

Colin Warburg

A Top Place

Because I came to study at Solent University, people from the department there came to the airport, Heathrow, and took me to a hostel here, in Marsh Lane. So I could just walk from there. After that I was behind Asda, where there is a hostel, right in the centre of the city. That was very good because one day I had water but no rice, but no problem, because I could see Asda and I ran over and got some! Asda is my top place.

Binu Vijayakumari

Veronica Tippetts, third from the right with the striped skirt, on an outing with fellow students from Southampton City College. (Courtesy of Veronica Tippetts)

Through to Finals

For me the first year was hard and it wasn't until the second and third years that I started to relax a bit more, go out and have more of a fun time. I am not sure that is what it is like today – they just start drinking straight away! You tend to work hard the first year, wind down a bit in the second and then a bit more in the third, even though you have your finals.

Colin Warburg

Through to Finals: Colin Warburg (centre) joining the ladies in their ballet routine. (Photo courtesy of Colin Warburg)

Farewell

Our lecturer was leaving so all of us got together, about ninety or one-hundred of us, in the lecture theatre and carried him out in a coffin. We had a thirty-year alumni meeting and I sent in one of the pictures I took that day.

Colin Warburg

Learning the Way

I studied software engineering. It was a one-year course but my dad died, so I made it two years. My home is in Kerala, in the south of India. If you go to some travel shops here you will see package holidays on sale because Kerala is full of beaches and there is what is called houseboat tourism. Basically you stay on a houseboat and you take the houseboat out, they catch fish from the boat and if you want to stop you can see houses on the side of the backwaters and you stop. It is all natural.

Studying at Solent was very good. My first impressions were very good. The course was not up to my expectations though. I got a scholarship – I paid only £1,500, which is very cheap for a masters degree, and I spent two years because my dad died in the first year. But the course was not as I expected. I cannot blame the university because my expectations were different. Assignments I had trouble with. Where I come from we have an assignment and we meet and discuss and then we write our assignments and they are all the same. Here, it is not allowed. It is called plagiarism. My tutor called me up and said I was copying. I said I was not aware of these things. In the first two weeks there was an orientation class and I was not able to attend that, but afterwards it was fine. I had to learn the ways of the university. I just used my practice from India but here it was not alright. It was a mistake I made. I failed a paper, but once I had an idea I caught up.

Binu Vijayakumari

four

LIFE IN SOUTHAMPTON

Rolling Mills

During the First World War, my mother worked in the Rolling Mills, Woolston, producing munitions. My mother wrote this about it:

A neighbour obtained a job in the offices of Rolling Mills and told my sister and I, named Leither and Leah Keable, that work was coming in, to make munitions. We applied for work and were taken on. The munitions came in with trained girls from Birmingham. Winter 1915/16 was the worst winter ever experienced. One wall and half a roof came down. We floated around on planks of wood – the whole place was flooded with water. At first only the nickel bullets machines were fixed first. They worked very rapidly. You had to keep your foot on a pedal, if not, the speed was so great, the machine seized up and all dyes broken. We often got a torn hand if the metal happened to slip accidentally. I won several War Savings Certificates for high output.

Moira van der Hoest

Racing for the Kaiser

My great grandfather, Captain Daniel Parker, used to race yachts for the Kaiser of Germany. He was a seriously famous sailor. When the First World War came along, he put his fingers up to the Kaiser and said, 'Stuff you, that is it.' He would not race his yachts any more. The Kaiser had personally asked him to race yachts for him before, and he did.

Geoff Parker

Captain Daniel Parker, sitting down next to the reclining man in front, on the Meteor in Hamburg in 1900. (Courtesy of Geoff Parker)

Bus Service

One of the things that might seem strange was that we ran a very good bus service to Hedge End. That is the original bus route that used to terminate at Forest Way, at the Peter Cooper garage in Hedge End. Hedge End never had a pharmacy. What would happen was that the people there would give our drivers their prescription and when the drivers came into Woolston, they would take them into the chemist and get the prescription filled and then take the medicine back. George, who worked at Thorneycroft, would go on Easson's bus. If George were missing they would pull up outside his house and bang on the door to find out where he was!

Ralph and Douglas Easson

Coach to Romance

They had cheapie trips from Southampton to Blackpool on the coach and one of these was where you travelled up on a coach all night, have the day in Blackpool and then stayed in a hotel before going back. I met Doris on the coach going up to Blackpool. It was one of the most uncomfortable coaches and it took seven or eight hours. We had the back seat and there were four big people on the back seat with us – if one turned, we all had to turn! She was with her sister. I always say you meet funny people up in Blackpool! We have been married now for forty years.

Jim Neal

Doctor Aldridge

Dr Aldridge, who lived with his family and had consulting rooms in Cumberland Place, at one time employed my mother (I think around 1923). Dr Aldridge was the first X-ray specialist in Southampton and important people came to him for consultations. Sometimes he would ask my mother to help set up the examination room, help with mixing the bismuth, moving equipment and other jobs. The patient took bismuth before being X-rayed. One patient my mother remembered well was Violet, Duchess of Westminster. She had a violet car with her crest on the doors. Her chauffeur's uniform was in a darker shade of violet. Dr Aldridge later died of X-ray cancer. At that time, little was known about the effects of receiving too much X-ray treatment, so doctors did not protect themselves as they do today.

Moira van der Hoest

To Fair Oak

Many years ago, our dad was driving one of the older buses through Fair Oak, down Craig Hill, which goes to where the Fishers Pond restaurant is. He was driving down the hill and a wheel overtook him and he suddenly realised it was one of his back wheels that had come off! It overtook the bus!

Ralph and Douglas Easson

An Elegant End

One of the bus bodies came to an elegant end: It ended up in Gran's Field. It was an old body that was taken off – an older chassis was re-bodied – so Gran had the old coach body put over in the field and turned it into the summerhouse.

Ralph and Douglas Easson

Dividing Line

Rownhams was where the nobility lived; Nursling was where the gentlefolk lived. We grew up with the dividing line and yet they were Nursling and Rownhams Parish Council.

John Sillence

Moving to Merry Oak

When my parents were first married, they lived in 'rooms' in Victoria Road, Woolston. They had to go through the landlady's living room to get to the kitchen, which was inconvenient. When Mum became pregnant with me, my parents went to the council offices to ask for accommodation, but there was no joy. Only when I was four years old and my brother Robin had been born, did my parents receive notification that they had been granted a council house. It was on a new estate called Merry Oak, Southampton. My parents thought they were in seventh heaven to have their own front door, back door, front and back garden, bathroom and three bedrooms. They were thrilled after managing in such cramped conditions for years.

Moira van der Hoest

Carnival

I was frightened sitting on the truck; health and safety wouldn't allow it now. I remember that people tossed coins at us. It was not pleasant. They usually threw them into the boxes, but they just threw them. They hurt. I was about seven.

Before we had the maypole put on the float for the carnival we had to learn to dance around it. We had to dance around with ribbons and I got terribly annoyed

Carnival time and the maypole has been hoisted aboard the truck. Seven-year-old Joan is sitting next to the boy on the seat beneath the pole. (Courtesy of Joan Shergold)

because the other children couldn't see that the dancing they were doing – they were supposed to be weaving – was forming a pattern around the pole but they couldn't see that. Every so often the teacher would say, 'Stop, you go back, you go back,' and she would unwind it, start the music again and then we would have another go. Everybody was out of step, except me!

Joan Shergold

The Floating Bridge in the 1950s

One day my uncle came to visit from Liverpool. He couldn't believe the Woolston floating bridge was free for foot passengers and bikes.

I used to work at Thorneycroft in Woolston. We had to leave dead on time after work in order to collect our bikes and cycle like mad to catch the floating bridge. Sometimes we would miss it, see it just pulling out, but we were pedalling so fast we couldn't stop in time and would ride into the River Itchen up to our knees. Other

The floating bridge with hovercraft in the background. (Courtesy of Ron Shergold)

times we would be on the floating bridge and watch others do the same thing and have a good laugh.

Bill Benson

Toll

When we ran the buses to the floating bridge we had to pay the Itchen ferry company a toll in Portsmouth Road, because where Woolston library is, down to the bridge, was a toll road. It belonged to the Itchen Ferry Company.

Ralph and Douglas Easson

When they were constructing the new bridge, the floating bridge continued to run and I remember where we lived in Sholing we did not actually hear it but where my boyfriend's family lived, in the high-rise buildings overlooking the river in Itchen, the noise from the construction went on day and night as the pile driver went down.

Christine Bagg

Gardening at 10 Cypress Avenue

Both Mum and Dad were keen gardeners. Mum had the front garden, and grew flowers, especially her beloved roses. She also loved pansies, verbena, hollyhocks, wallflowers, sweet peas, stocks, and nasturtiums. We often had Nasturtium leaves in salads – they have a taste similar to watercress. Dad had the back garden, which was mostly taken up with vegetables, his specials being runner beans, beetroot, carrots and onions. In his greenhouse of coloured glass Dad would bring on seeds in boxes until ready for the garden. But the main products were his tomatoes and cucumbers. I loved tomatoes then – and still do. Dad's tomatoes were wonderful – special – the smell and feel of them. Supermarket toms aren't a patch on my Dad's toms.

Moira van der Hoest

In the front garden at 10 Cypress Avenue. From left to right: Leah Mortimer seated with husband Arthur standing behind, their daughter Moira with granddaughter Eleanor on her lap and Dutch husband Niek behind her, and Niek's parents, over on a visit from Holland. Note the pansies in the lawn. Leah loved her garden. (Courtesy of Eleanor van der Hoest)

The Changing Police Scene

We were coppers, now they are officers. There is a subtle difference. I joined in 1952, which was then Southampton County Borough Police. Nobody in the force had a degree at all. We had virtually no political interference. The Home Secretary used to be the position that was responsible for policing as a whole. I could arrest an MP or another Chief Constable or the Mayor without qualms and no problems. If I thought he was drunk in his car, I could lock him up and there would be no pressure from anybody. We were all practical coppers and we were all living in Southampton.

We had a beat system. We had four police stations, which were manned by police officers 24 hours, seven days of the week, every day of the year. Now, you have only one police station, which is open 24 hours. Of the other three, one is closed completely, and Bitterne and Shirley are closed of an evening and civilians, with no police background or training, man them. It makes a big difference when you go in to report something. We had vehicles within the city boundary. Each station had an emergency driver with a transit type vehicle whose job was immediate response to any treble nine calls within the division – Shirley, Bitterne, Portswood or Central. In addition to that, each division had a divisional motorcyclist, who worked eight to four and four to midnight. I was one for a couple of years. They were out on patrol within the division in eight-hour

Coppers, not officers. (Courtesy of Jim Brown)

Police Constables on parade.
(Courtesy of Jim Brown)

Jim Brown directing the traffic.
(Courtesy of Jim Brown)

shifts, to respond immediately to a treble nine call. Each station had two vehicles at its disposal to give an immediate response within the division. We also had five traffic cars and fifteen traffic motorcycles all on traffic duties within the city boundary. You had all those vehicles for immediate response, which is why there was a directive from the Chief Constable at that time that if an officer was not at the scene of a 999 call, not answering the call but at the scene of the incident, within four minutes of the call, a report had to be on his desk the following morning with an explanation. We were there within four minutes.

Southampton was divided up into forty-six beats and there were beat officers. You had to ring in every hour. When you were reporting for duty you were told, 'Right, you're ringing at five past, you're ringing at ten past', and so on. So, each station would have twelve to fifteen men going out, two until two, two until ten, and ten to six nights. Also, there would be a 5 p.m to 1 a.m. shift and an 8.30 to 4.30 shift. You had a five-shift pattern so you had double cover a lot of the time. All the beats were covered by foot patrols; you didn't have radios in those days. We patrolled on our own. We coped. We didn't have to have a buddy with us all the time. On the beats at nights you would check all the properties and all the front doors of all the shops and the back alleyways, and the back of the premises. None of that happens today.

Policewomen

Policewomen had a very low profile. There were only a few policewomen and their function was mainly to deal with statements for sexual offences or women with young children, or searching women prisoners. They only had ninety per cent of a man's pay. You wouldn't consider them going on the beat on nights on their own.

Nip Things in the Bud

We used to nip things in the bud. All the pubs were seen out. You get all the trouble now with drunkenness with the students and down the High Street at night with yobs. It was quite simple in my day - if people were a bit boisterous no problem, but if they were drunk and disorderly they were locked up. If they were drunk and incapable, they were locked up. On television you see now that doesn't seem to happen much. It is accepted. It has got beyond control really. I feel sad when I see in the *Echo* sometimes, shopkeepers on parades of shops being plagued by yobs who are causing problems. It didn't happen in my day because when it started to happen the shopkeepers made a complaint and the man on the beat the next day would be told. He would go and see to it and sort it out. It is too trivial for the police to attend now.

Amalgamation

It was in 1967 that Southampton and Portsmouth amalgamated with Hampshire. County policing is totally different to city policing. It took a long time for the County people to realise the urgency of dealing with things and nipping things in the bud in the cities. We used to call them carrot crunchers and they called us city slickers. At that time, the Southampton City Police Force was 525 strong. In January 2009, in the annual Police Review online, it was 490. That is why you don't have beat men.

Beautifully Bound Book

One of the first things that happened after amalgamation was there was a new Street Offences Act that came out. The authorities, in their infinite wisdom, decided that there should be a Prostitutes Caution Register. Prostitutes had to be cautioned initially and it was only on the second caution that they had some sort of procedure toward them. To do that the force brought out a beautifully bound book for the Prostitutes Caution Register. You could not have a loose leaf file one because naughty detectives, who had prostitutes as informants, might take the pages out or might remove the evidence, so it was properly bound. I was in the Civic Centre when the sergeant said, 'Listen to this lads, I am going to phone headquarters.' He called them and it took quite a while to get through to the right department who had issued the book.

'Sergeant So and So here, can you send us another Prostitutes Caution Register?'

'You had one last month.'

'Yes, we need another one.'

'My god you haven't lost it? You know how much they cost.'

'No, we have filled it up!'

It proved a point; they had no idea of the administration of it. The daft thing was, this beautifully bound book went to every station, so Netley would have had one, Hythe would have had one – they didn't have any girls on the game. Southampton Central had one, the same as all the rest.

First Arrest

My first arrest was as a young PC. I had only been in the job for a few weeks. I came out from Shirley police station, walked down Shirley Road to go down to my beat and there was some waste ground, it was an old bombsite. It was overgrown with grass. As I walked along, I saw children playing around there. I saw someone lying down in the long grass and I thought that was a bit strange. One of the things about being a copper is you are nosy, you are inquisitive. So I strolled across and there was a chap with his trousers down, exposing himself. So I arrested him for indecent exposure. I charged him with 'wilfully, lewdly and openly exposing your person contrary to …' and all that. When a person is charged and he is cautioned, no matter what he says – it could be an obscenity or absolute rubbish - no matter what he says, it has to go on the charge sheet. So the Station Sergeant takes the charge and says, 'Have you any reply to the charge?' and whatever they say goes down. His reply to the charge was, 'I've got TB and my doctor told me to get as much fresh air as possible.' It was my first arrest. It did not wear at court. He got fined at court, just the same.

Talking about stop cases, I was called Lucky Jim. I was walking down to my beat and a chap was walking towards me. It was in the afternoon; a crowded Shirley Road with lots of people about. He walking towards me with a boiler suit on and carrying a big holdall, and he caught my eye as he approached me. I looked at him and I thought he looked a bit iffy. I stopped and checked him. I went through the routine: 'Sorry to be a nuisance my friend, do you mind telling me what you have in your grip?'

'Not much.'

'Can I have a look? It was chock-a-block with loose tobacco.

'What is your job?'

'I am an electrician.'

'Where do you work?'

'British America Tobacco in Millbrook.'

He came into the station. The thing is, when you arrest anybody, the first chance you get you have to search them. So down in the station I said, 'Now take your boiler suit off, I am going to search you.'

'No, I am not going to take my boiler suit off.'

'Well, you are. I am asking you, take it off. If you don't, I will get somebody else in and we will take it off.'

'Do I have to?'

'Yes, you do. I want to search you.'

When he took it off I saw why he was reluctant. He had a black brassiere on, black silk stockings and suspenders and panties, he was a complete transvestite underneath. There was no offence, of course; he was not breaking the law but he was embarrassed. I was not embarrassed – you get used to it.

A Girl in Trouble?

When I was a young copper in the fifties, a similar thing happened. Marian, my wife, and I had bussed into town. We lived in Sholing and had gone to the pictures and came back on the late night bus. It was about 10 p.m. and we got off the bus at the top of Northeast Road. We crossed the road and as we started walking down we saw a woman walking towards us on the opposite side of the road. As the car headlights lit her up, I could see she had a turban on and a blouse and she had a skirt that was split right the way up and you could see the top of her leg. She saw us looking at her.

'Look at that, she's got no skirt on really,' I said to Marian. The woman turned around and walked into the copse behind her. It was ten at night and she was going into bushes and shrubs. I said to Marian that there was something wrong and I was going to go and check her. So I crossed the road and I hurried along the path and she sort of broke into a little trot and so I called out, 'Don't worry love, I'm a police officer, there's nothing to worry about.'

'Well, that's all right officer,' came the deep, bass-voiced reply – it was a bloke! I brought him back. He had underwear on and had a beautiful pair of breasts - really striking! Although it was no offence, there is a possible importuning for immoral purpose. Also, there are the sorts of people who pinch stuff off clotheslines, so I had reasonable grounds for detaining him. I said to Marian to go on home. I phoned up the station to pick him up. While I was on the phone, he was taking his shoes off. Then he's doing a runner down the road. I left the phone dangling. I soon caught him because I was very fit in those days. I dragged him back forcibly and a couple of other people at the bus stop stared; as far as they were concerned here was a bloke dragging a girl along, saying, 'Don't you get away from me.' This poor defenceless woman! Anyway, I got him to the police station and, again, I had to search him. He was reluctant. He had two balloons filled with water in his brassiere! Apparently, he was married with two young children and his wife did not have a clue. His wife went to bed early and he would dress up in her clothes, put makeup on and go out walking for a little bit.

Jim Brown

History

At five years of age, I started school at Middle Road Infants' School, Sholing. Four years ago, while helping children with reading problems, I mentioned to a member of staff that I had started school there in 1932. The next day she presented me with a photocopy of the register with my name entered in it. History!

Moira van der Hoest

Passing the Test

Our first buses were Model T Fords. In those days you never had a Ministry of Transport; they were inspected for roadworthiness by the Chief Constable of Southampton and they had to be taken to the police station. The company had one off the road because they had weeds growing through the back seat. The seats were stuffed with straw. They could not afford the horsehair so they went for straw.

Ralph and Douglas Easson

SRS Southampton

The Sea Ranger Squadron Southampton was named after naval ships called HMS *Southampton*. Not that long ago the last HMS *Southampton* was decommissioned, in 2009. There were five *Southamptons* before that. The ranger unit started in March 1943.

I joined at the age of fifteen in 1958. The reason I joined was that my father was in the Royal Navy and I wanted to join the Wrens. But he said, 'No. I am not having my daughter in the navy.' My cousin happened to be in the Sea Rangers and so I thought, that sounds good. I joined and we went to regattas in Portsmouth, rowing what we call Montague Whalers. It had a point at both ends. The oars are fifteen or sixteen feet long, which meant that you didn't sit the same side as the oar goes out of the boat, you sit at the opposite side. As you rowed them, the oar went 'twing' because of the length of them; they had a fantastic spring on them. Consequently, it needed five people and a cox.

The first Easson coach – a Model T Ford. (Courtesy of Ralph and Douglas Easson)

Pat Tarry is on the left next to the boat. The new Montague Whaler Aquarius is about to be launched from the slipway on the corner of Priory Road and Adelaide Road, St Denys. Pat's sister, Joan, stands to her right. (Courtesy of Pat Tarry)

Canberra

We decided to do a sponsored row in Southampton Water and we went to the Western Docks. Our little boat tried to row past the *Canberra* - you can imagine how big she was compared to our little sixteen-foot boat. We took over three quarters of an hour to row past her because of the tide, which was against us at that point. In the end, the police launch, *Ashburton*, felt sorry for us so took us back round the Itchen. They towed us to the boathouse. Our whaler was called *Auriga*. All our boats were named after a constellation.

1939

SRS Southampton is based at 288 Broadlands Road. It will be knocked down and will be a division HQ within the next three years. We had a gas man come and look at the meter. He said he was looking for the number on the meter. 'Do we have numbers on the meters?' I asked. 'I can't find one on here,' he said. Then he pulled away a bit of stuff and he said, 'Do you know, this gas meter is dated 1939!'

The Boathouse

The boathouse was down by Cobden Bridge. We had a little jetty. We then went to Priory Hard, which was next door to Belsize Boatyard, Priory Road. We share with the scouts a three-garage boathouse there. First of all we had a little shed farther around the corner for it, but they wanted to develop the hard and so we got moved from there.

Accounts

My father enjoyed my being in the Sea Rangers and he was embraced into it. If the hut needed anything doing to it he came along and he would do it. He just didn't want me to join the Wrens. He said it was not the life for a girl. So I just had to accept it. I worked in an accounts office in Eastleigh for thirty-two years and then for another company there for nine years.

Pat Tarry

SRS Southampton hut, 1970. (Courtesy of Pat Tarry)

Pat Tarry has been guiding for half a century. (Author's collection)

Fairey Aviation

As my dad had not finished his apprenticeship when he was called up into the military, his employer, Thorneycrofts, was obliged to take him back to finish it at the end of the war. As soon as his apprenticeship was finished he was dismissed, as there was no work in shipbuilding. Staying on the subject of work (jumping ahead a bit), it was some years later when he found employment at Fairey Aviation at Hamble. He stayed in this job until he retired at age sixty-five. He used to cycle to and from work daily, until after the Second World War, when Fairey arranged lorries to transport workers to and from work. My dad was collected and dropped off at the top of Lances Hill.

Fairey Aviation had a repair depot at Eastleigh Airport and my dad was among those who were transferred there during the Second World War. He was not called up then

The Thorneycroft generations: seventy-seven-year-old Arthur Mortimer (seated) on a visit to Thorneycroft, where he served his apprenticeship in 1913, his son Robin (in white) who began his working life at the company as a shipwright apprentice in 1943, and grandson Nigel, who was a metalworking apprentice. Arthur's father, Samuel, also worked for Thorneycroft, having moved with the company to Woolston in 1906. (Courtesy of Eleanor van der Hoest)

because he was doing essential report work to fleet aircraft. My dad was a very good workman, very reliable.

Moira van der Hoest

Redbridge Rehabilitation Centre

Between the ages of thirteen and twenty-one I had thirty surgical procedures. The surgeon who did my last operation said, 'Joan it is time we did something about your future. I can get you on to a rehabilitation course for the disabled and once you have a green card you are guaranteed work.' I could not keep a job. If you were ill you were out of your job. I was cured of what I was ailing and it was time for me to be trained properly. So I got on to that. In six months, we were to learn what it took other people three years to do in college. The course was superb. I got up at six every morning and caught a bus to Redbridge. We started at eight and we stopped for breaks and we got paid while we were doing it. And we got the green card. I was taught so well that I left there and got a good job. I aspired at that point to be a managing director's secretary. I could see that was a nice job to have. Then I met Ron and that put paid to that – I became an army wife.

Joan Shergold

A class learning shorthand and typing at the Redbridge Rehabilitation Centre. (Courtesy of Joan Shergold)

4 per cent Interest

We started looking for a place of our own to live. Most places advertised were snapped up quickly and we couldn't find anywhere suitable to rent, so we decided to buy a house. Fortunately, I had a marriage gratuity from work (Post Office Telephones). You paid contributions into a fund, deducted from your salary. On getting married you received a lump sum, which could be used towards a deposit on a house. We looked at several houses and the only one we liked and could afford was on a new development in Portsmouth Road, Sholing, Southampton. We made enquiries and obtained a mortgage from the council (Southampton Corporation).

The interest rate was a static 4 per cent which was marvellous. The house price was about £2,100. The gratuity wasn't enough for the deposit and my dear dad – bless his heart – lent us £50 (a lot of money then). Every Saturday Niek used to go to my parents and pay off an instalment on the loan until he had paid it all off. My parents thought the world of him and respected him very much for this. Dad kept a card on which he recorded the weekly payments.

When we put our names down for the house, it hadn't finished being built. We used to go there every week to see how much work had been done. Niek was so proud because he was the only one in his family to buy a house.

Moira van der Hoest

The Dolphin Hotel

I first stayed at the Dolphin when I was awarded a Fulbright Scholarship to go to the USA and I sailed on the old *Queen Elizabeth 2* in the late fifties. I returned to Southampton a year later on the old *Queen Mary*.

I next stayed at the Dolphin in 1972. I unearthed a postcard of the hotel, a very handsome one, which I sent to my late husband, telling him I had got that far – there had been a serious rail strike and passengers had been advised to get to Southampton early as ships could set off at any time! I had Chispa (Spanish for 'Spark') with me, the Golden Retriever puppy I had bought while at the University of Liverpool finishing my dissertation research, and the Dolphin was wonderful about letting her stay. I recall that opposite the quaint old lift we used to creak up and down in, there was a tall mirror and she would ALWAYS bark at herself, vastly amusing other guests!

I say on my card, postmarked June 1972, that the Dolphin was 'Very nice and central'. I also say on my card, 'It's cold, grey, wet. I am still in winter clothes!' The card

Proud new homeowners – Niek and Moira van der Hoest. (Courtesy of Eleanor van der Hoest)

The Dolphin Hotel. (Courtesy of Julie Green)

shows the Dolphin with a red double-decker bus in front and the caption reads, 'High St, looking North, Southampton.'

I finally sailed on the *France*, French line, and a ship and crew from Hell! Surly, nasty, disobliging – it was that ship's last voyage so perhaps that influenced things. Oddly, though, they did have a printed Menu for Dog Meals on board, including an item called '*Vegetarien des Chiens*'.

Tessa Nelson-Humphries

The Fishing Boat and the Liner

I often went fishing with my granddad Keable. One day, I had gone fishing with him and my dad – I must have been a bit of a tomboy! We were fishing in the fairway (special canal dredged to allow big liners to come up into the docks) and the men didn't notice this huge ship bearing down on us. We shouldn't have been in that area. It was the *Berengaria*, the then flagship of the Cunard White Star Line. You get an awful 'wash' or wave, when these liners go by. I clearly remember a man with a megaphone at the ship's rail shouting, "You bl★★★★ fools – aren't we big enough to see?' Of course, passengers were standing along the rails, too! The men were scared, so was I. We all lay on the bottom of the boat while it went up and down like a cork. Afterwards, we made our way back to Swift Road. When Granddad related our mishap, Grandma was so angry with him – I remember her saying, '…risking a child's life like that!' I don't remember if we caught any fish that day!

Moira van der Hoest

The Panel Club

Before the war, there was no National Health Service as now. People used to pay so much each week into a 'Panel' club. Every year, we had a carnival in this area, the money going to support the Royal South Hants Hospital. Everyone took part, it was the same as our City Carnival these days. This particular year, Mrs Veal, from Magnolia Road, put in a lorry with the tableaux of Mary, Mary Quite Contrary – Nellie Veal was Mary, her friends were the flowers. We were all called to the Head's office, as permission had been asked for us to leave school early to prepare ourselves in our costumes of crêpe paper. I, fortunately, was a simple tulip. Others were given slightly more difficult names. I remember Doris Watts was a Chrysanthemum. There was also

Moira's grandfather out on his yacht. (Courtesy of Eleanor van der Hoest)

a Geranium, Peony, Amaryllis and so on. I think Doris got her spelling right, as we all had to spell our flower names before we were given leave to go.

Moira van der Hoest

Very Naughty

I did something very naughty to obtain that picture. I stole into the Southampton Docks. I nipped past a policeman or two with my camera because this is the *Aquitania*, the last four funnelled ship. They don't look like ships anymore but I desperately wanted to take her picture, and there she was. It was taken about 1948. She was just finishing her life. She was the last one with four funnels in existence. She was the same as the *Titanic*.

Douglas Brown

The *Aquitania* in Southampton docks. (Courtesy of Douglas Brown)

Cox's Cut

If you go over the Central Bridge and just go to the left and underneath, there used to be a big cattle market where they used to kill the cattle. Also, for the cattle that came from the other side of the town, they would pen off the floating bridges into pens, which got the cattle across the water. The back of Lloyds bank in Woolston is known as Cox's Cut. That was the name of the big butchers in Woolston. Cattle were walked along the Cut and were killed there. Our grandmother remembered seeing it all and she said she used to put a stick in their head and stir their brains up! That was Grandma!'

Ralph and Douglas Easson

Weston Beach

When we visited my maternal grandparents, who lived at 2 Swift Road (the last house before the shore at Woolston), Robin and I wore our Sunday best clothes. I wore a white dress, white socks and white sandals. Robin and I were sent out for a walk. We wandered down onto the beach. The men had been digging for bait (for fishing). They had left piles of mud and stones next to the holes. Robin and I began jumping from one pile of stones to the next.

We were some way from the shore when it happened; I slipped and fell into a hole filled with black, smelly water. The more I tried to get out, the more stuck I became. Frightened, I called out to my brother to go and fetch our dad. Robin scrambled up the beach and disappeared. I knew enough that I must remain as still as possible until help arrived. Suddenly, my dad and granddad appeared dressed in overalls and carrying two planks of wood. First one plank was laid on the mud and Dad crawled along, bringing the second plank. When Dad reached me, he put his arms around me, under my shoulders and heaved. Two or three more tries and suddenly I was free, minus shoes and socks. My lovely dress was ruined, torn, black and very smelly. Dad picked me up and carried me home, while Granddad retrieved the planks of wood.

Grandma's house had a scullery with a low clay sink. Here, I was stripped of my clothes and washed off. My mother's sister Lily lived nearby, at 14 Weston Grove Road, and she had a daughter, Edna, a year younger than me. Robin was sent to Aunt Lily's to borrow a dress. I suspect he was asked for a pair of pants but forgot. So Robin was asked to let me have his pants to wear home! My dear Dad carried me home, piggyback style. All this time, not a word of blame or reproach was spoken. Next time we visited Grandma and Granddad, Robin and I were sent into the front room to read a book – we couldn't be trusted, that was punishment enough.

Moira van der Hoest

Meet the Family

My father went to sea like all the family. They were all seafarers. My mother's brother was on the Union Castle and he met my father. He invited him to meet his family. My mother's father had Italian roots, the family name being Giacomelly. Her father had gone off to the Boer War and changed his name to Smith. That is how my father met my mother, Ruth Smith – bang! That was it. They were married in 1949 and I was born three years later.

Geoff Parker

Ruth Parker (*née* Smith). (Courtesy of Geoff Parker)

Ben and Ruth Parker on their wedding day in 1949. (Courtesy of Geoff Parker)

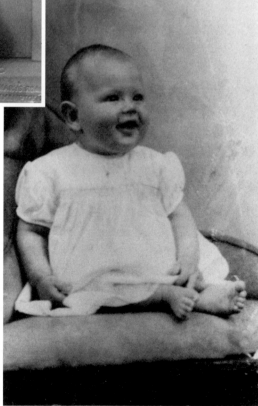

Geoff Parker – a beautiful baby!
(Courtesy of Geoff Parker)

Bittersweet

I grew up in Sholing, at 66 Kathleen Road. The present owners have just taken down the hedges, which I used to hide behind with boyfriends, and have just put a brick wall up. It is totally changed. They have an extra bit on the side of that place. I bet they never queried it – my dad moved the fence up. The neighbours said, 'You'll get into awful trouble.' Mum went for him. Nobody has every queried it and that was fifty-five or sixty years ago. There was a rough track to the fields at the back to Alfriston Gardens but if you look at the house, you can see it has a wide garden.

I got married from there, to Brian, who was also from Woolston. Our Golden wedding anniversary was bittersweet as he has dementia. I took him all through it, asking him, 'Do you remember when we got married?' I reminded him about the marriage service, who married us, and where we went for honeymoon, and he sat there and he said, 'I can't remember.' On the day, although he enjoyed it, and enjoyed the people, and we had a tape with 1950s songs on it; it was bittersweet, it really was. Brian is far worse now.

Carol Cunio, Mayor of Southampton, 2010/2011

Brian and Carol Cunio on their wedding day. The bride made her gown, which cost £4. (Courtesy of Carol Cunio)

Strawberry Fields

My father's father and my grandmother lived in a small house in Ruby Road but my grandmother's father had actually owned all the land around where Itchen College is now, as well as on the other side of the road to it. It was all strawberry fields at one time. The land was sold off sometime in the 1920s as there was no money in land at all and he got virtually nothing for it, I think.

Christine Bagg

The Choral Union

In 1945 my mother and I joined the Southampton Choral Union, later known as the Southampton Choral Society. Mr Ambrose Chalk was the conductor. My mother and I were both first sopranos.

The ladies wore long black skirts and white blouses, the gentlemen dress suits.

In 1947 our conductor, Mr Chalk, announced that we were to perform Handel's Messiah from the Southampton Guildhall in December as usual. And it was to be broadcast – such excitement! Previously it had always been the Halle Orchestra, or London choirs or orchestras who had had the privilege. The orchestra would be the BBC Symphony Orchestra, with its well-known conductor Leslie Woodgate. The soprano soloist was to be Isobel Baillie, with other famous singers singing the alto, tenor and bass solos. The organist was George Thorben Ball. It was a very impressive list of names.

We practiced and practiced. The great day finally arrived. There was an afternoon rehearsal with the soloists. All went well, and Leslie Woodgate said we made a good 'noise', which we were told was BBC jargon for a good sound.

The Civic Centre clock was stopped for the occasion, so that the concert would not be interrupted by the bells chiming the hour.

It is a great feeling standing on stage at the Southampton Guildhall, looking down into a packed hall. My mother had bought herself a special copy of the score of Messiah. In the interval, my mother decided she was going to get her copy of the Messiah autographed. I said I didn't think time would allow. But off she went. She returned absolutely triumphant! My mother, in the short space of time, had obtained the conductor's signature, also that of the four soloists and organist – plus every member of the BBC Symphony Orchestra! I was truly amazed, as my mother is not an autograph hunter. No one else in the choir had thought of it.

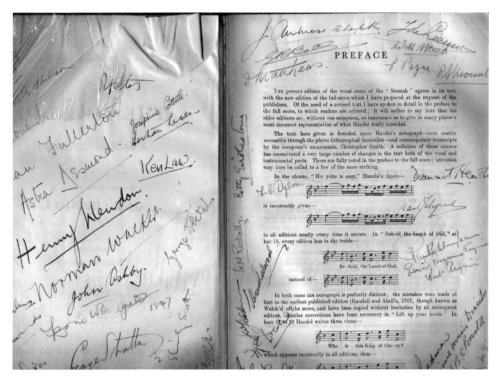

The opening pages of the score of *Messiah*, covered in autographs. The BBC Broadcast was a huge event in Southampton life. (Courtesy of Eleanor van der Hoest)

When the *Echo* came out with the report of the concert, my mother cut the article out and clipped it in the front of her copy of the score. I have the book now and when Christmas comes around, and the BBC broadcasts the Messiah, out comes my mother's book, and I re-live the memory of that evening.

Moira van der Hoest

Cadena Café

I remember a lot about Above Bar because I used to work in an upmarket store there, Bourne and Hollingsworth, window dressing. I could see the world go by but particularly I remember the Cadena Café (later the Jolyon) because you used to get such gorgeous cakes in there, especially the rum babas! There was always a big queue of people in there. It was quite a big coffee shop.

Penny Cox

The Best

If, and when, we went shopping on Saturday into town, we would sometimes buy pork sausages from a shop called Northovers in East Street – they were regarded as the best.

Moira van der Hoest

Mini Skirts

The 1960s was the decade of the mini skirt, so the dresses were quite short. Long dresses were also fashionable and I do remember a very nice pink one I had, glittery at the top with a scoop neckline. It was empire line and went down to the ground. Men all wore suits.

Elizabeth Streatfield

Southampton Common

The Common and the graveyard were so big and scary and I had never been to a graveyard like that. It was one of the biggest Victorian graveyards in England and I found it really strange as I lived in a little village then and was on my first visit to Southampton before we moved to the city. I thought, *Ooh, let's get away*! When we walked through the Common it was huge – 365 acres – and I remember we walked around the Common and it was my birthday and I thought how weird the Common was.

Jackie Early

Our Wedding Day – 9 January 1954

The wedding was booked for 1.30 p.m. at Peartree Church. The Civic Centre clock was just striking half past one as Dad and I got out of the car at the church.

On the way to church, I said to my dad, 'I suppose you're going to give me some advice?' He said, 'You've got a good man there. You're young enough to have fun and old enough to be sensible.' I always treasured these lovely words of his.

Mum had been to see the organist beforehand to arrange the music. She asked for '*We'll gather lilacs*' (Niek's and my favourite song) but he didn't want to play it as it wasn't church music. My mum said, 'I'm paying, you'll play what I ask.' So I entered the church to the music of 'We'll gather lilacs' and Niek was waiting for me at the chancel steps. As I came up the aisle, he turned and smiled. I was very happy on my wedding day. Mum and dad approved, which was wonderful.

After the ceremony, we had photographs at the church before going on to the reception. I had previously arranged for a phone call to be made to Niek's parents (at home in Holland, unable to attend the wedding) so he could speak to them on his wedding day. This involved booking the call a week beforehand (no direct dialling then) and arranging for the charge to be added to the baker's bill, which we repaid later, as we did not have a telephone. It was the same baker who made the wedding cake.

The waitress answered the phone and announced that there was a phone call for the bridegroom. Niek grabbed my arm wondering who could be phoning him there. We both went to the phone. I remember Niek saying, 'Yes, I am the bridegroom.' He spoke to his mum, dad, Jan, Gerrit, Jannie. Unbeknown to us, his family were holding a reception at the same time for us in our absence – what a lovely idea. I said hello to Moe and Vader. It was quite a celebration. When Niek realised the call was my doing, he drew me to him and kissed me, and said what a wonderful thought it was to arrange the call. He was choked with emotion. It was a very happy reception. I heard Niek say, 'I'm a married man, I'm a married man.'

At about 6 o'clock, we went to Southampton Central railway station, still in our wedding clothes. My cousin Derek, who was in the Royal Navy, asked the station master to broadcast an announcement offering congratulations and best wishes to the newly married couple, Mr and Mrs van der Hoest. People on the platform started clapping and cheering.

Moira van der Hoest

The Dawn of Computing

When I did my postgraduate degree it was at the advent of computers and PCs. My colleagues were very keen on that and I ended up financing the purchase of a couple of PCs, which at that time were quite expensive. I had an electronic typewriter and kept having to start again. With a computer you could put everything in and if you made a mistake you could just edit it, then print it out.

I had a number of colleagues who were doing vivas and I did quite a lot of pieces for the friends I had. We were quite pioneering on that side. We also starting talking

Moira and Niek's wedding day, 1954. (Courtesy of Eleanor van der Hoest.)

to local companies and seeing what they needed, and one of my colleagues did programming. I learnt programming – in those days it did not take very long to learn – and we started to do programmes for people. When I completed the PhD, I did two years as a Research Fellow. At that point, we were working on what we could do with PCs and how we could make that work. In fact, after two years of Research Fellowship I left and went off and formed a company, Cerver US Software Ltd, which I then ran for about twenty-odd years. It was quite a boom time for the computer side.

One of the first programmes we wrote was for a double-glazing salesman in Southampton. We must have sold twenty or thirty copies of that. At that time, we would write every one individually. You take the design and size of a window and from that comes your cutting list. The double-glazing salesmen were taking a day or so to calculate each window and the computer could do it in seconds. It was an easy sale. At that point, I realised that if you want to make money on computers you don't write a programme once to sell it, you write it once and sell it many times. We went on to do that. The progress was fast and we peaked with Swift messaging, which is bank-to-bank messaging.

Colin Warburg

Tony Blair

When I arrived in Southampton I did not know a single person, so I thought if I fall in trouble that the best people to start with would be from the church, so I went to the New Community Church in St Marys, near Marsh Lane and met a lot of people. I knew Tony Blair through TV – that was the only person I knew in the UK.

Binu Vijayakumari

Methodist Manse

Funnily enough, the house my husband and I used to live in was the old Methodist Manse. People don't know it was a manse but there is a house on the corner of St Albans Road – opposite Itchen College – and that was the Methodist Manse where the minister used to live. We bought that and lived in that. It used to be owned by the Methodist church and the minister used to run the church that my father and grandparents and great-grandparents used to go to. How local we are!

Christine Bagg

Southampton Family

My mother Josie (*née* Hanlon), who was known as Molly, was local to Southampton. Her sister Annie Wade had two children, Michael and Eileen.

Eileen, was mentioned in Dispatches in the War because she rescued a Polish Jewess. Eileen Wade's married name was Caborn. Her mother Annie lived in Bernard Street, eventually becoming the longest inhabitant in the road. Annie's other sister, my aunty Mary, lived round the corner just opposite the pub that was in Orchard Lane. She owned a second-hand shop she called an antique shop.

Michael married Rosie in the early 1940s but Rosie died young, leaving two children. Eileen took the baby, Anne, and brought her up. Anne Caborn went to school in Romsey and she was a journalist on the local *Echo*. Micheal and his mother Annie kept the other girl.

Veronica Tippetts

Eileen Wade, mentioned in the Second World War Dispatches for heroism. (Courtesy of Veronica Tippetts)

Micheal and Rosie Wade on their wedding day. (Courtesy of Veronica Tippetts)

Pong!

The Corporation collected vegetable peelings and there was a man came around and it was taken away. They used to make these big cakes of pig food from the vegetable peelings. The smell, the pong – we shut the windows when they were making it if the wind was in the wrong direction.

James Marsh

A new Career

I was lucky, I was thought of highly– I was one of the first scene of crime officers and one of the first motorcyclists. I was keen. In 1968, I was sent for and I was asked if I wanted to start up a crime intelligence bureau. I was given an office in the Civic Centre and a couple of PCs and it was a question of being collators. People would give us information. We would have information of every prisoner who was arrested, his vehicle and that sort of thing. We had no computers. We had a card index system and I devised a system. For example, for every vehicle I had four cards – one for its colour, one for its make, one for its numbers and one for its letters. It meant that if we had a dark Vauxhall or part of a number, we could find it.

I got bored. I was an office worker and it was interesting but I was dealing with other people's stuff. I was then thirty-eight and I had eighteen years' service. It was made very clear that for further promotions they wanted flexibility of people moving about and they wanted to merge the city/county attitudes. My roots were in Southampton. I was approaching the age of forty and that was a magic number for employers. When you turned forty you were over the hill and you had to turn to a new career before you were forty. That is what I did.

I was lucky. I got in on the ground floor of a massive consortia of consortiums – all the major shipping lines in Japan, Germany and England had got together to form container lines. In the UK it was called OCL – Overseas Container Line. Containers were in their infancy, American. They were going to start the new container terminal in Southampton, called Solent Container Services, and I was one of the first half dozen in the company. I was offered the job of Chief Security Officer, which I took. I went to the Chief Superintendent and said, 'I am putting my papers in, Sir.' He said, 'Don't be a bloody fool, you're talking nonsense.' He couldn't believe it. Marian thought I was mad. But I knew what I wanted. The force was changing. It was not a family anymore.

We had no terminal; the terminal wasn't built. We took photographs, which are

Jim Brown was one of the first police motorcyclists. (Courtesy of Jim Brown)

unique now, of the terminal being constructed. I was stepping in for the administration manager, responsible for the entire canteen, cleaning and maintenance staff. I helped with the security aspects of the terminal – the locks and the furniture. I had my own office and my own security staff. I interviewed my own staff and my pay was more than I was getting as a Sergeant. I had a good pension scheme and I could work until I was sixty-three, whereas I would have had to retire at fifty in the police, with thirty years' service. I enjoyed it.

Jim Brown

The container terminal under construction. (Courtesy of Jim Brown)

The container port in action. (Courtesy of Jim Brown)

Jim Brown in his office at the container terminal, where he was Chief of Security. (Courtesy of Jim Brown)

The Queen's Silver Jubilee

When it was the Queen's Silver Jubilee, we had a street party just around the road, because it is a very small estate. We lived in Tenterton Avenue and the street party was in Dysart Close. All the people who lived in that area joined in. We all had to wear hats that we designed to do with the Jubilee and my children wore hats that were like cakes. I think I made it from cardboard and painted it and put candles on top. There were no prizes. It was just for the fun of it. Then there was a big, long table down the close and all the children sat round the table and the adults just made sure everything was OK. We all had decorations up in our houses, the Queen and the Duke of Edinburgh, and Unions Jacks. There were Union Jacks around my cake hat!

Jackie Early

We lived in an area of semi-detached houses and in 1977 there were lots of street parties started to be organised for the Silver Jubilee, so someone set up a committee and they called on all the houses in the area to do a street party. It was so successful a Community Association started. Eventually, it folded up because it was always the same people doing the hard work, but for a couple of years we had good events. We had a barn dance and a tramps ball one night. A family walked all through Portswood with an old pram and they had soaked themselves in reeking onions! Some really good things came out of that Jubilee.

Glen Jayson

The Cinemas

There were so many cinemas in the city. There was the Classic cinema, which was in the High Street – we used to go in there and smoke in the back seats, I remember doing that. Then there were three others. I remember the organist man who used to go down and come up playing. The Gaumont was where the Mayflower theatre is now.

Jackie Early

On Sunday afternoons the people used to go to the cinema and there were queues all around as they waited to get in. There was no television then.

Veronica Tippetts

Bins

You put the bins out the back door, never out the front like you do today.

Elizabeth Streatfield

Football

My husband, when we were boyfriend and girlfriend and he wanted to give me a treat, would pick me up from the library and we used to hotfoot it to the Dell. I remember once we got there too late and they had scored two goals by the time we got there!

In 1976, Southampton won the Cup and everyone came into Southampton to celebrate. I dressed the children up. My little one was in a pushchair, she was only about eighteen months, and I dressed her in red and white! It was quite exciting as everything was red and white. They have gone down two divisions since then, haven't they?

Jackie Early

The first year I was at Southampton was also the year they won the FA Cup. That evening a lot of celebration took place in the town, including at the Red Lion, where people were hanging from the balcony!

Colin Warburg

Welcome Here

We did a thing called 'Welcome Here'. It was about women from all kinds of ethnic minorities, French women, American women, Pakistani women and an Indian woman, there was a nice woman from Belfast, an Italian woman and a Spanish woman – in all about twelve. We took photographs of them, talked to them about being here, talked to them about their life here. It was to emphasise that they were welcome here. We enjoyed it and it was part of Woman's Week – it was a fortnight then. I was teaching then, in 1996. I did a project every year. We had an exhibition in the Civic Centre.

I have lived here thirty years and I like being part of a different community. I like being part of a multi-racial society and I was also repaying a friend who did a favour for me. Each year, we did a different project and one year we did one on clothes. We had the Bargate but, unfortunately, it was only open one day a week so not many came to see it.

Mo Foster

O.G.S. Crawford

There was a big house on Redbridge Lane, they have pulled it down now, and there was a guy in there who you could never get to answer the door. He sent his lady in black out. His car broke down one day somewhere in the city centre and my dad said he would fix it. My dad said that his son would like to have a look round the man's gardens. The lady came round and said that I could come in, but not go in the house. The man was Mr O.G.S. Crawford from the Ordnance Survey – he was inventing a way of surveying from the air. My father told me that he would be changing the way they do the maps. I spoke to him once. The trouble is, at that age, you don't know who on earth people are, or their significance.

John Sillence

St Mary's Street

We used to have T Ford chassis and one of the bodies we had put on one of the chassis's was made in St Mary's Street. They took the chassis along St Mary's Street and the body was made in an upstairs workshop! They lowered the body out of the window on to the chassis.

Ralph and Douglas Easson

Pleading

Then the back axle and the half shaft went. We have a letter at home, in which our grandfather, Douglas Easson, is pleading for a loan of 10s so he could stay in business. It is dated early 1921 – we know the business started in 1920 – and it is basically a begging letter from Dad's father to his First World War friend Bob Essex, who was still in the army at that time. It is basically saying that the back axle has gone again, it is going to cost two pounds, twelve shillings and sixpence to put right – which he did not have – and it was saying, I have to feed the kids, so … It was the way it was addressed that was interesting – it was his best friend – not 'Dear Bob', but 'My Dear Essex'. That was the way things were done.

Ralph and Douglas Easson

The Libraries

I worked in the library in Southampton and that was quite interesting. When I was at school I was going to train to be a librarian. I was going to do a year in the libraries before going to college, so I started off in the Central Library. I came home on a long bus journey every day so it was quite a business really, what with the hours and everything. I was going to do a two-year course to be a qualified librarian. One of the things Central Library had to do was to fill the other libraries with staff. Quite often I would be sent out.

One day they said, 'Woolston need staff, off you go.'

I said, 'Woolston? Where's Woolston?'

'You find the floating bridge, there is a little hut, and you go over. Here's your fare.'

I was really, really upset about it as I didn't know where I was going. So I got on the bus and went down and had never seen anything like the floating bridge and the little hut that you waited in. Just what is this place? I thought. I remember when I was coming back I said to them, 'Can I leave a quarter of an hour early because I have to go all the way back to Waterside.' They said, 'Oh, we will see.' They did let me go early. It was interesting being sent out. Shirley is on its third library that I have worked in.

It was quite interesting because that was the first time I saw Asian or black children. They came to the children's library. They came from a different culture and I was so unused to it. The children all had the same surnames. The girls were all called Kuur and the boys were all called Singh, so that was the names we used. It was useless in the library because we had hundreds and hundreds of the same name.

I worked in the big lending library where you discharged thousands and thousands of tickets – it was not computerised. You had to go through the whole issue.

We used to have to wake the tramps up. The tramps would come into the reading room. We were instructed to go behind and drop big books to wake them up. You weren't allowed to touch them or manhandle them out of the library but we were not going to make it comfortable for them. So, if they fell asleep you were instructed to go around and drop the biggest dictionary you could find on the floor behind the tramp. So you did that quite a lot to get rid of them. They were very smelly. They sat by the radiator and the smell that came off them was just awful.

Jackie Early

No Shops

Between Nursling and Shirley I don't think there was one shop. We had to trudge across fields to get to Shirley. I jumped on the tram in Shirley – that was our main transport. It was wonderful – the noise of rumbling over the track and the speed. When they started up they got up to speed fast and when you got to the end the driver unhitched the power thing from the top and turned it around so that you could go back. That was the main journey for me – from Shirley terminus where Sainsbury's is now down to the Royal Pier.

Old Great Grandfather Hurst

Gradually, my open space between Nursling and Shirley became built up and built up. Lordshill was last. In the middle of all this was one poor guy, Old Great Grandfather Hurst, who had a caravan and a three legged dog and no way was he going to move

A view of old Shirley, 1905. (Courtesy of Julie Green)

The Royal Pier in 1925. (Courtesy of Julie Green)

and so they built round him! Eventually he had to move. His relations still run a farm and shop in Frogmore Lane.

John Sillence

Writing Group

I had two writing groups for the WEA – the Women's Educational Association. I had a friend and she involved me. I worked with underprivileged women in Gosport, that was lovely, and then I started writing. I was on a course for Channel Four and I got the job through there. I did it for about fifteen years (which is far too long), at the Argyle Centre in Landguard Road. Several people went on to get published from my groups. They were feminist groups. It was wonderful. We went to Greenham Common.

Mo Foster

The Rose Gardens

The Rose Gardens were where tours went from, right in front of the Civic Centre. Behind were the Hants and Dorset bus station and the Grand Theatre. The fountain, which is now outside the library, was situated there, right in the centre. Everyone knew the Rose Gardens, and would meet there.

James Marsh

Christopher Cockerell

A bloke called Christopher Cockerell was working on a hovercraft in Southampton so he came to my dad and said, 'Well, you've worked on the Spitfire, want to work on the hovercraft? The first ones you couldn't even get into but then he managed to get between the Isle of Wight and Southampton. He gave us a bunch of free tickets. We got so sick of going! I had a drawer of free tickets and in the end Mother said, 'I don't think we can go any more over to the Isle of Wight.' In the end, I think we ditched them!

John Sillence

The Lido

The Lido was where Leisure World is now. We used to come over on the ferry from Hythe. There was another pool, we are talking about the fifties or early sixties, not the pool we have now, but it was expensive so you would walk past that pool, past Pirelli's, and you would get to the lido, which was outdoors. It was freezing! I suppose the water used to come in from the sea. It was a nice place to go and it was cheap, and it was great fun. When you are little you don't care about it being cold, do you?

Jackie Early

We used to go to the Lido for the day and take bread and dripping.

Veronica Tippetts

First Impressions

My first visit to Southampton from Scotland was in 1954 when I was nineteen years old. My boyfriend of three years wanted me to meet his family, who lived in Northumberland Road. He had been evacuated to Scotland to live with his aunt when war was declared and had lived there since.

We had to get my Grandmother's approval before setting off as that's how things were done.

My first impression was of the central station being so colourful, as there was a red carpet on the platform and flowering hanging baskets in abundance. I didn't think this was on my account and we learned later that Princess Margaret, too, was visiting.

I was very impressed with the city; the old walls, the museum and the parks with their crest-designed flowerbeds. We had ice cream in the Cadena café and watched the tramcars go by in the High Street below. The warm sunshine enhanced everything and I noticed that most of the houses had their doors painted different colours.

I believe the Lido open-air pool had just opened and we spent an afternoon there where, fascinated, I watched a family enjoying their swim. It was the first time I'd seen anyone with black skin and the lady was wearing an orange coloured swimsuit. I was intrigued to see that the little boy's tight curly hair didn't look wet as he emerged from the water.

I sent a postcard home comparing Scotland to Southampton, saying that it was like stepping out of a black and white movie into a Technicolor one and I loved it.

Jean Thompson

Veronica Tippetts (left) and her sister Betty at the Lido. (Courtesy of Veronica Tippetts)

Carol Cunio receiving the Whitbread Care Award in 1989. Carol was involved with church projects in Southampton and throughout the county. (Courtesy of Carol Cunio)

The Churches Together

I was the Ecumenical Officer for Hampshire and the Islands – The Churches Together. The whole idea was to get churches locally to work together and pray together and do things together and I really worked so hard on it. In lots of places it took off. I did it for eight years. I produced a huge newsletter every quarter, which I had to post out to everyone. I gave advice on how to work together. I would travel a lot. I went visiting places – the Channel Islands, the Isle of Wight – it was good. I said to them, 'Look around you, what can you do for the churches in the community – it's not about shutting yourself away in the church, go out there!' Winchester churches, for example, started helping with the homeless and that is still going on.

I always say church is outside. At Christmas time, the Mayor always has a Christmas carol service in the foyer in the Civic Centre. I said, 'No, I want to take it outside. I want to take the Christmas message out into the streets.' We had people from the Sholing Salvation Army band there. It was a freezing cold evening, and what a turn up. I had a very good plug on Radio Solent – the Mayor wants to take the Christmas message out on to the street. That did it. You could see people walking by, stopping and listening, and then walking on. The next Mayor may not want to do that but the manager at the Civic Centre said that if he does not want to do it, we could still do it. I thought that the churches could do it – get it organised. I was really pleased with that.

Carol Cunio, Mayor of Southampton 2010/2011

The Altar Cloth

After the 1939-45 war, when rebuilding was started, an appeal was made by St Mary's Church in Southampton, for gifts to help refurbish the church. The church had been badly damaged by the bombing and was almost a shell.

My parents made an offer of a lace altar cloth for the Seaman's Chapel, which was accepted. Together, my parents set to work with the design. My father designed the lace. It had a Calshot lighthouse in the middle with its rays of light. Also there were ships, flowers and church symbols worked into the pattern. My mother made the crocheted lace with the finest Irish linen thread. At last it was finished and the day of consecration came in June 1956. Queen Elizabeth (the Queen Mother) was guest of honour. My mother was at the service. My mother had also made a lace altar cloth for Peartree Church Lady Chapel.

Many years later, when my mother was housebound and in her eighties, she would talk about St Mary's altar cloth, and wonder if it was still in use. I decided to find out. So one evening, I made my way to St Mary's Church in Southampton for evensong. One of the sides-men was a gentleman I knew from the Head Post Office. He asked me what I was doing there, knowing I lived across the river. I told him about my

St Mary's altar cloth, still in use at the Seaman's Chapel. Designed by Arthur Mortimer, it depicts the Calshot lighthouse. The crochet work is by Leah Mortimer. (Courtesy of Eleanor van der Hoest)

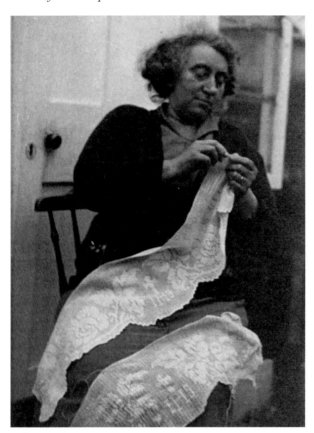

Leah Mortimer at work on the altar
cloth for Peartree Church. (Courtesy
of Eleanor van der Hoest.)

parents' gift of the lace altar cloth in the Seaman's Chapel, and how my mother was
wondering if it was still in use. He said, 'Yes, we still use it, in fact my wife launders the
linen. Wait after the service in the Chantry Hall and I'll introduce you.' Afterwards I
met his wife, who, when she heard why I was at church, asked if I would like to take it
and show it to my mother. I said, 'Yes, please.' So after ten or fifteen minutes, the lady
handed me a brown paper parcel and asked if I could let her husband have it back by
Friday, this I promised to do and thanked her for the kind thought.

On Monday after work I visited my mother. As I didn't usually go on that night,
she was curious as to why I had come. So I asked her to shut her eyes and hold out
her hands. This she did and I placed the brown paper parcel into her hands. When she
opened her eyes, my mother said, 'What's this?'

'Ah,' I said, 'I know, and soon you will know.' Slowly, she undid the brown paper,
then came a plastic bag, next was the tissue paper. As my mother unwrapped the tissue
and she saw the lace, tears came into her eyes.

'How and where did you get this?' she said. 'I never thought I would see it again, and so well kept.' I explained my mission, and the kindness of friends. In those days (before it had to be returned), my mother had many visitors, as she told friends and neighbours about the cloth and was able to show her and my father's handiwork.

On the following Thursday after work, I visited my mother. She told me to thank my friends, especially the lady who laundered the cloth and kept it so beautiful. So the altar cloth was returned, from a very happy lady.

Moira van der Hoest

In the Docks

The dockies had their own language – they referred to each other as 'My Babe'. They had nicknames and despite the fact that the press always gave dockies such a bad name, we actually worked in the docks probably for eleven years, driving buses about. When they were trying to unload the car ships, we would drive the dockies from the car compound when they came off the ship, back to the ship to get more cars off. In all

Dockers by HMS *Amazon* at Southampton docks. The ship was commissioned in May 1927. (Courtesy of Eleanor van der Hoest)

the years we worked there, we never had a problem. They were very nice people, but interestingly, the dockies had a whole way of life. They were very charitable people, no one ever knows that really. Lots of money was raised for the children's cancer ward for example and for a special party for deprived kids.

In the shipyard everybody had a name. You could not do it any more, because political correctness says you can't. One bloke was called Beano. Why was he called Beano? Because he only came out once a week! There are hundreds of names like this and they have all gone.

Perks

In the old days, when the cargo was manhandled, part of the dockies' perks was a box of almonds, which they would split. They had chilled meat and pigs come in. Once, when some of the dockies wanted to nick a pig, they got a car and they dressed the pig up in a coat and sat it on the back seat with a cap on its head. There were three people sat in the back of the car and the middle one was the pig!

Ralph and Douglas Easson

Southern Electric

I went and lived in Woolston for a while and I had to go over on the floating bridge every morning to go to work at Southern Electric. I got a job with the civil service when I was sixteen, but I wasn't allowed to join them because Her Majesty required my services. They were going to keep my job. I stayed on at school and then got called up.

I came out of the army after two years in Germany and was in Southampton. Southern Electric had a place in the Bargate. On the window it said about interviews for a job. Of course, I had not put an application in. That was Friday when I looked at it. It was accountancy. A bloke came out – who turned out to be the chief accountant – and he said, 'You interested?'

I said, 'Yes, but you're doing the interviews today.'

'Have you come out of the army?'

'Yes.'

'Have you a CV?'

'Yes.'

'Let's look at it. Oh, this is better than the people we've had in. When can you start? Monday?'

That was my interview, on the pavement outside. I started Monday. My first job was behind the counter taking money and then he asked if I wanted to come up to his office upstairs and learn accountancy, which I did. Forty-four years later, I retired.

John Sillence

Babe in Arms

We met at school. We married when I was a babe in arms. We have our fortieth wedding anniversary in a couple of months. I saw a ruby ring I liked and it said 'Price on application' so I applied. It was £47,000, which was only just over a thousand pounds for every year of marriage!

Jackie Early

The Mons Moonbeams

My mother, Ivy Neal, had a concert troupe, the Mons Moonbeams. My mate and me used to do the Punch and Judy show in our spare time. We all went to carnivals in Hedge End and Botley. The concert troupe had a chorus line of girls; it was before the TV came in. It is a very small world. The year before last my wife and I were up on Lake Windermere and we sat down with this young couple that came from somewhere in the Midlands. We said we came from Southampton. He said, 'My parents came from Southampton. They used to belong to a concert troupe there.' I said, 'Well, that's my mum!'

Jim Neal

The Civic Centre Fountain

The Civic Centre fountain was when the city was really nice, really fantastic. It was in the middle of the gardens over where Matalan is now, and the traffic went around it. It was right in the middle of the road and it was all lit up in the night-time. It was really lovely. That was moved in the mid 'eighties.

Geoff Parker

Swinging

Sixties Southampton was a swinging place to be. I lived in Chandlers Ford and I was betwixt Southampton and Winchester. In Winchester there was nothing going on. We always went to Southampton.

Elizabeth Streatfield

Plested Pies

The Plested pies today don't taste like the original Plested pies. We can remember going over to a Plested pie shop, which used to be round by the old Hants and Wilts bus station in Windsor Terrace and there was about twenty women who used to work in that place. They would be rolling out pastry, filling it and putting them in the oven – everything was done on the premises. Something special was the way you eat them – so you didn't end up with gravy all down your chops.

Ralph and Douglas Easson

Memories of St Luke's

I first started at St Luke's when I was thirteen or fourteen, when my parents moved from Southbourne, Bournemouth, to become caretakers at the Temperance Institute, 30 Carlton Crescent. I was soon in the choir, having started my treble singing at St Katherine's Church, Southbourne. Both churches were Anglo-Catholic, St Luke's more so than St Katherine's.

The parish priest at St Luke's was Canon Father H. Douglas Caesar, a parish priest in the old way, who had served the people of the parish all through the Second World War. When I joined the church, together with my family, it was still in its bombed state. The western end of the church had been hit with a bomb, which destroyed the bell tower, leaving a big hole and a porch, which led nowhere. The church bell had to be pulled with a wire strop running out through the wall.

The church was never much 'in favour' with the Diocese of Winchester, because of its being Anglo Catholic. We never at St Luke's talked of the 'Eucharist', let alone the 'Lord's Supper' – 'Mass' was said daily – on Sundays at 7 a.m., 8 a.m., and High Mass (the Tridentine form) at 11 a.m., with Evensong and Devotion to the Blessed Sacrament at 6.30. There was a thriving Sunday school and a good choir. My voice

Douglas Brown (fourth from the left, in front of the rail, beside the man in the black jacket) and the St Luke's Choir. (Courtesy of Douglas Brown)

didn't break until I was nearly seventeen, then Father Caesar taught me to sing bass! Boys' voices broke much later in those days. These days a church would give its right arm to have a choir as big as St Luke's choir was then. I still sing in a choir, in West End.

Outings

St Mary's, St Matthew's, St Mark's, St Mary's South Stoneham and St Augustine's all had huge boys' choirs as well as St Luke's. The lads all came along – they knew there was going to be an outing and a few of them would leave this church in order to get there in time for the Mass at St Matthew's and their outing, or St Peter's for their outing – whipping out of one set of choir robes into another! By and large, they were loyal, but that sort of thing did happen, especially in Sunday school. There would be a mass entrance into ours when it was going to be the Sunday school outing and a mass exodus when it was going to be St Peter's or St Augustine's! They were children and, of course, they wanted plenty of treats. I don't blame them at all – I was one of them, doing exactly the same sort of thing! I went with the other boys of the choir to outings in the summer, to Ryde and the Isle of Wight and to Hengisbury Head, amongst other trips.

Outdoor Crib

When I was about sixteen, Father Caesar asked me to create an outdoor crib with some cardboard crib figures he had been given by students of the Southampton Art College. I was happy to do so and made a crib scene out of the outside porch. There was a pipe sunk into the ground for people to put donations into. A lot did so but many another just threw coins into the straw of the crib. There was no attempt to vandalise it, nor the church, which was always open for people to pray in.

St Luke's outdoor crib. (Courtesy of Douglas Brown)

Going around the Pubs

At Christmas time, we boys, in our robes, would go with Father Caesar and our choirmaster round the pubs in the parish singing Christmas carols and getting a welcome from the drinkers!

In the summer, we would go up onto Southampton Common and have an open-air service there, quite near what is now the United Reform Church.

Every Thursday morning, I would serve Mass and then go on to school. I served the altar and learned to be an altar servicer. I went to the church until I went to university, when my family moved away. When I came back to Southampton I was dismayed to find it not in existence as a church anymore.

I am still a Christian and would not be had it not been for St Luke's. I am so very grateful for Father Caesar, Father Burl and Father Swinerton, the priests there.

A Saint

To me, Father Caesar was like a saint – I absolutely adored him. As a parish priest he was an ace, what you think about being a parish priest – serving his people at great personal cost to himself. He put himself out for them, the church and the faith, and he was a great priest teacher.

Douglas Brown

Getting Married

I had a lovely wedding. It was at the church in Onslow Road. It is a Sikh Temple now. It was St Luke's Church. We had a very nice ceremony in 1966. I just stood at the altar, my brother beside me, and I waited until she was suddenly there and that is when I realised. I couldn't believe it was happening. She was wearing a traditional long white dress. We went from there up to the Target, which is now defunct as well. It was at the end of Bursledon Road and we held the reception there for sixty people, with a traditional wedding cake. We went up to Blackpool for a week for our honeymoon. We moved into a flat over my favourite fish and chip shop then. I had been looking everywhere, the wedding was coming up and I went in to buy a bag of chips. The owner said, 'Have you had any luck flat hunting, Jim?' I said, 'No. It will be my mother's front room.' He said, 'Come with me' . He took me upstairs and there was this lovely

Canon Father H. Douglas Caesar, the popular priest of St Luke's. (Courtesy of Douglas Brown.)

flat, it had a titchy little kitchen and bathroom, and a bedroom and a lounge. It was £1 12s 6d a week and so we had that, and then we moved into a maisonette the next year, when our son James was on the way.

James Marsh

Married Life

We were married at St Patrick's. We were very broke, so it was a little, tiny wedding. I made my wedding dress, which cost me £4. We went to the Isle of Wight for our honeymoon. Then we went to Leicester, where Brian was working, and we were five years there before we came back. He was a computer consultant, having gained a physics degree from Southampton University. He went straight into computers. In those days, computers filled the whole room, you had to put in the punch card things, which I still have a few of, somewhere.

When our eldest son Stephen, who is also into software and computing, said he was second generation, they did not believe it at work and then he explained what Brian had done.

Carol Cunio, Mayor of Southampton 2010/2011

On the Buses

I was a bus conductor for the Hants and Dorset buses. I was on the buses when the people came to Calshot, off that island, Tristan da Cunha. [In 1961, there was a volcanic eruption on the most remote inhabited archipelago in the world. The islanders were evacuated to Merstham in Surrey and then on to Tristan Close, Calshot.] They were there off the remote island where they had no roads, nothing and you can imagine the uptake when they came over here – they had no television. They were living in the RAF camp in Calshot. They were all sheep farmers. The ladies used to wear these thick white woollen socks and all their clothes were wool. They were lovely people. The girls were going to school and you would notice that they started wearing a bit of makeup. Most of them went back (1963) but one or two stayed over here. One of the drivers married one of the girls. He had to go and see their leader, for permission to marry her.

Jim Neal

Northumberland Avenue

I have lived in Northumberland Road for thirty years. There are far more Asians here now and there is the mosque just down the road, which is nice. They had a gorgeous Imam before. He always talked to my dog – 'Hello dog, how are you?' I feel safe because there are always men going in and out. They are very friendly.

There are beautiful kids in the Asian community. From what I can see they are much more gently treated and loved more, especially boys. The girls are little housewives. I think they value children more. That might be a sweeping statement!

Sikh Funeral

When my partner died, they took me to a Sikh funeral. It was very interesting. All the women went in one room and howled, which was excellent. I joined them. My partner had died and I was terribly upset. All the wives kept saying, 'Get a grip', but they said, 'Don't get a grip.' It was sixteen years ago, but some of them still come up to me and say, 'Are you alright?'

Mo Foster

Hello

Coming to England was my first time abroad. I think Southampton is very good. I spend a lot of time walking around because I spend time in the library and when I finish I think, why not? I walk at night a lot. Tomorrow I need to be in London at 9.30 in the morning. I am taking a bus – I think it is not too bad – it is leaving at 6.30 but sometimes it goes 5.30 and that means 5 o'clock I walk. I don't have a car and every day, if possible, I try to walk to see the local life. To be honest, it is very good. It is not like big city London. The people are fine and the thing I like most about it is, now I am nearly going to be in my tenth year here, every time I go out anywhere I will see someone who I know and I say 'Hi.' Imagine if you are in London or Birmingham, the person will knock you down if you are in the middle of the park! That is one of the things I like. They say, 'hello' and that is fine.

Colder Climes

I arrived here in September so the weather was all right but people started to scare me – 'Wait until December!' But it was not too bad, to be honest. I met some senior Indians here and they said that in the past, when they were young, there was always cold but nowadays nothing. I did not feel any discomfort. I feel acclimatised now.

Binu Vijayakumari

Chantry Hall and the Ice Rink

I am now in property development. I was going to restore the Chantry Hall and build flats with retail and office space and we were also going to make the first zero carbon building, but the government changed the rules. Chantry Hall had a fire and got burnt down and now that it is where I am going to put the ice rink for Southampton. It will be a tight fit but it will go. I had initially looked at the ice rink two years before, next to Jury's Inn, 60–64 St Marys Road, which is owned by the council. I went to them and asked if we could put an ice rink there. The council wanted to go through as a tender because it was a public space. We came in slightly under the highest spender but we were providing £15m worth of sports facility. The leader at the time, Art Samuels, said to me he would not support it simply because he was going to go for the highest bid. I said what about the community. His quote at that time was, 'I don't give a damn about the community,' which did not impress me. They then sold it on to a housing association, which was going to put houses on it. The idea of bringing sport there was to bring the community together.

I was working on the Chantry Hall project at the same time. I had always seen them as two separate projects, the Chantry Hall and the flats. We had removed the QuickFit and garage and got planning for a triangular building on there. We had a couple of million coming from Heritage Lottery but when the hall got burnt down it added a million pounds to the costs to restore it. It was not good value for money and so, after six months, we had to delist it and demolish it because it was unsafe. It was then that I realised how big the site was. On paper I had only looked at it as two sites, I had never looked at it as one. Now we are a couple of years further on and we have planning for it. I hope we will be opening in 2012. The café could be run by social enterprise; local people running it. The money will be retained within the community. It is an exciting project.

Colin Warburg

Richard Parker

A young cabin boy, my grandfather's cousin's son, Richard Parker, signed up as a cabin boy on a yacht bound for Australia. There was a cargo on board and there was the captain and another three or four crew, which were all that were needed. The yacht blew off course, went down in a gale and they all got in a lifeboat. The others ate Richard.

A couple of years ago, I was in the art gallery just looking around and the Nuffield people were there, re-enacting that scene. I heard them chanting 'Richard Parker' and I went up and said, 'I am an ancestor.' They just stood still and looked at me with their mouths open. They called everybody over, about twenty players, and they said, 'This is an ancestor of Richard Parker!' Andy Warhol said everyone is famous for fifteen minutes – they just stared at me! They re-enacted the story down in the old law courts and the woman in charge asked if I would come to the performance. So I went down and there was a crowd of people and they sat me in the courtroom where whoever is on trial used to sit. I sat there for two hours watching this and all the people were

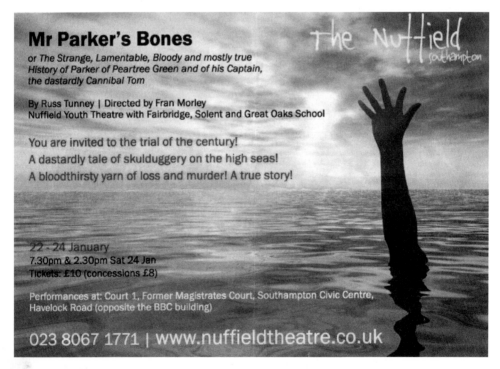

A flyer for *Mr Parker's Bones*, the dramatization by the Nuffield Theatre of a horrible true tale of cannibalism. (Courtesy of Richard Parker's relation, Geoff Parker)

looking at me, wondering why I was sat there. I have never done anything like that before and I suffer from embarrassment terrible. I am sat there and at that end of the show the one in charge announced, looking at me, that I was a descendent of Richard Parker. Everybody then understood.

There is a memorial to Richard in Peartree Churchyard. It is on its side now at the back near the railings by the road.

Geoff Parker

No View

The main changes I am seeing is that people used to sit on the balcony in the seating area in West Quay and people come there to see the sea. Now Ikea, Carnival and the hotel are there and in two years the car park area will be gone. So all the big buildings are blocking the view. I don't know what will happen to the boat show. I have been to it a number of times. I think that after some time, there will not be enough places for it. More flats are coming. Sometimes I don't think this is very good, but we need to think about people who need housing.

Binu Vijayakumari

Fresh Air

I like to walk along Weston shore. Fresh air is always good. In my place (India), I get fresh air 24 hours. Here, I get one hour. I am always inside. That is bad. That is the very bad thing that happened in my life. The first month I came here, my hair started to fall out. So, when I go back to my home it does not fall out. I went for blood tests and checks and they can't find anything. The water is different, sunlight and fresh air – so when the sun is out I go for a walk and it is getting better. Fresh air and sunlight is the only difference to home, so I spend time walking in lonely places. I walk to get sunlight and fresh air. I sit with my head in my hands so that I can get the sun on my head!

Binu Vijayakumari

Carol Cunio, the Mayor of Southampton, at the Southampton Care Home, Portsmouth Road, pictured with staff and Vi (left) a resident. (Courtesy of Carol Cunio)

Art

Southampton is a football city and it is getting better culture-wise all the time – we have one of the biggest art collections on the planet and that is fascinating and that just goes to show you what this city used to be like. I always think it should belong to Salisbury or Winchester.

Geoff Parker

Mayoral Duties

I visited the Southampton Care Home in Portsmouth Road in January 2010. 'They wanted to see me, so I popped in. One of the residents, Vi, took a shine to my driver! It was so funny.

Carol Cunio, Mayor Southampton, 2010/2011

five

THE WAR YEARS

The Rolling Mills

The Ministry of Munitions set up rolling mills in Weston during the First World War. Percy Hendy's was Britain's first Ford dealer. The original Ford production line was going to be at the rolling mills and after the Great War, when it was no longer used for making munitions, Henry Ford wanted to buy that and make it the first production line. The idea was to ship the cars from the US, across the Atlantic, in crates, in what is called 'completely knocked down kits'. Hendy used to assemble them into cars. The authorities would not let them build the Ford place here and that is one of the reasons it went to Dagenham on the Thames.

Ralph and Douglas Easson

Yanks!

The US Troop trains were wonderful. They were a gift to us because food was so short and we had powdered milk, not fresh, and things like that. But when a troop train came down, there was a signal on the railway line that was just across from our back garden and the cry went up – 'YANKS!' And we came out of our houses and over the fence because they were throwing things out to us – tins of food, fruit, chocolate; things we could not get. It was cascading down the railway bank and we kids, having left the adults far behind, were all there with bags picking it up. It was shared with the people of the road. So when the cry of 'Yanks!' went up, it was grab a bag and run. Every house was doing it. We knew what to do, pick up as much as we can and shove it in the bag! They had so much and we had so little, and they knew it.

James Marsh

Thornhill

I was born in Thornhill Village, not Thornhill, in Mons Crescent. I can tell you a bit of the story of Mons Crescent. The guy who built the bungalows in Mons Crescent and the houses in the road was in the battle of Mons (1914) and he was a colonel in the army. He built all the bungalows, houses and a few of the shops in the original village. In the 1960s there was no Thornhill estate or airfield. The airfield was Edwin Jones' Farm. Thornhill was a big place. In those days you could go and play in the woods without worries about children being molested.

Thornhill was a proper village. It was outside the boundary until the Thornhill estate was built in the early 1960s. Thornhill was all woods. There was a massive army camp there. I was only about eight or nine at the time. There were American and English soldiers and they used to come down to our street at night from their tents – they were living in tents up there – and have a bath and a cup of tea. We knew what they were there for, they were ready to go over to Normandy and one night they came down and my mum said, 'You're a bit quiet.' They said, 'Well, we are not here tomorrow.' We knew then they were going. The sad thing was, we knew that one or two survived but some of did not. Us kids used to go up there and sit on the tanks! There were tanks all over in the woods!

Jim Neal

Jealousy

My parents, Percy and Josie Peet, and my sister Betty and I were bombed out when Coventry was blitzed in 1941. We came to Southampton in 1944 and settled in 63 Denzil Avenue. Then we went on to Germany as father was in the Royal Army Medical Corps. I can remember in the Denzil Avenue house that my mother's bedroom was the front room and I was cross when my father came home because she moved me out. I did not see why I could not sleep in bed with them! I was jealous of this man who had come back – and he would not give me his medals! I was about six. We sorted it out though.

Veronica Tippetts

Spitfires

My father, William, was working with Mitchell, the Spitfire bloke at Vickers. He worked for Vickers and Mitchell said, 'I am thinking of making a plane. You're working on planes, would you like to work with me?'

Mitchell looked up in the air one day and saw a bird, a swift, coming down, and he said, 'That is the only way to beat a German plane – something like that.' So he set to work on the Spitfire and my father had to work every night – never daytime, always night.

The German people were always trying to bomb them out. They never succeeded and so my father got through the war.

All the American pilots had to come over and learn all about the plane. My mother, Rose, did their washing so they gave me gum, which was the best chewing gum you

Veronica Tippetts (*née* Peet) and her elder sister Betty. Veronica was told by the photographer to 'watch the birdy' and remembers getting very upset as there was no 'birdy' to watch! (Courtesy of Veronica Tippetts)

could get. She cooked a meal and did their washing. A lot of the pilots gave their wills to my mother and said that if they didn't return from the war she was to post them on. A lot of them ended up in concentration camps in the end. I was only five or six at the time, but I was told afterwards that some never made it back and Mum had to post their wills to their relations.

Smart Americans

The Americans' uniforms were so much smarter than ours – they had money put into it. They enjoyed the English food but I never realised the significance of it – why they used to come over. I was a small child.

John Sillence

Air Raids

When we lived in Shakespeare Avenue, Portswood, we had to go to St Denys School in the air-raids on our own.

Sheila Cornwall (née Cox)

Air Raid

A coach company, Summerbee's, ran a coach to Overton on Sundays for the parents to visit the boys (who had been evacuated). The idea was that the coach would leave when the boys went in to tea. On this particular Sunday, when I had gone with my parents to visit Robin, one fond mother wouldn't leave until she saw her son after tea and held up the coach. Consequently, when the coach arrived in Southampton, the double red alert had sounded and the planes were overhead with a lot of noise. We alighted from the coach with hosepipes all over the place, holes, etc. and started running down St Mary's Street where everything was on fire.

My parents and I took refuge at the Six Dials air-raid shelter, right alongside the railway line. There were about thirty people there and some children, among them a man with an Alsatian dog. The dog was very friendly and quite soppy. The children were playing with him and ruffling his ears and so on. After some time, an ARP (Air Raid Precautions) warden came into the shelter. On seeing the dog, he immediately ordered the dog out. 'Not allowed,' he said in a loud voice. He soon had his marching orders from the people, as the dog was causing no problems and was taking the children's minds off the dreadful row outside. This was the night that Edwin Jones (now Debenhams department store) had a direct hit and was on fire. The shelter opposite in Hoglands Park also had a direct hit. The shelter was filled in and left as a communal grave.

When the all-clear sounded, we emerged from the shelter to see a sky reddened by fire, acid smoke in your nostrils. My mother, father and I walked home, through Northam, over hosepipes, dodging bomb holes, over Northam railway bridge, along Bitterne Road, through Athelston Road, up Cross Road into Chessel Avenue. Along Spring Road, there were trees down and holes in the road. Our house was still standing, but had a huge crack down the outside wall. We were lucky to be alive.

Moira van der Hoest

Belgrave Road

I was born in Southampton in Belgrave Road, which, when I look at pictures of it now, looks like it was a slum. It was not like that. It was a community. It was the sort of place that you were privileged to be in. Even though the times we had were pretty hard, we made our own fun.

Most people had an Anderson shelter in their garden, even my grandmother did in Mayfield Road. They were set into the ground and were then covered in tin, so you dived in there. We didn't. We had these great big brick shelters and the reason for this was because the major London railway line ran right by the back of our houses and they were a prime target. So bombs dropping there would have dropped straight on us. But it never happened. Bombs dropped nearby and how we got away with it, I don't know, and why Belgrave Road was built next to the railway line will always be an issue.

Just one incendiary fell on us, and that landed on the one space in the road that didn't have a building. The man who defused it, Mr Eldridge was the only man in the road who had a telephone. He ran the Belgrave Boys Club and he also looked after the church hall. He was really the leader of the road. He immediately raced down and defused the bomb. I don't know how he got the know-how to defuse the bomb but he rendered it useless. It was about 200 yards from my house.

James Marsh

Messerschmitt

I had to go to school in the war. The planes always came over and circled Nursling –
that was where the run in to Southampton was. As we walked to school, the planes
were circling and we walked through that. They went and bombed Southampton but it
was excitement to people of my age. One day I got so excited when this Messerschmitt
came along. My grandfather said, 'Dive in that ditch, that's a German thing, get into
that ditch!' He did. Not me. I went all the way up the road waving to the pilot. This
pilot came straight for me. He got to me and he tipped his wings to each side and
soared over my head and went and bombed Southampton.

John Sillence

Memories of the Veracity Ground, Sholing

The Veracity ground has a very interesting past but during my lifetime I remember it
well during the Second World War. We lived opposite the Veracity Ground and there
were swings and roundabouts on it. On Dunkirk day I opened the curtains and saw the
whole of the Veracity Ground was full of dirty and dishevelled French and Belgium
troops, they filled up all the schools. The community got together. My mum had eight
children so we didn't have much to give them but she cut a bar of soap in half and gave
that. After a few days they went up to the north of the country.

One morning we woke up to a noise and there was a barrage balloon and airmen.
One day the barrage balloon blew away. After that the Royal Air Force had a 40mm
gun that shook the whole house.

We moved from there and after that the American army camped there.

Joan Smith (née Cox)

The Southampton Blitz

The first bomb fell on the art school in 1940. I was in the Royal South Hants Hospital
at that time. It was very relevant to me, as I had been destined to go to the art school
myself. Here I was, ill in hospital. The bomb was a direct hit on the Civic Centre.
It went right down through the art school and into the cellars. In the cellars were
the shelters where the people were sheltering. They had the steam pipes down there,
which heated the whole of the Civic Centre and of course, all the children went down

there. They were scalded and burnt and all the children that went down to the shelter were killed. I don't know if there were any survivors or not. I was in the ward when they were brought into the hospital and that was a story in itself. The patients went on strike on that day. They would not eat anything until the children were looked after. I always tell that story and read it, because I have it written down for the City Archives. It makes me feel very emotional indeed.

The most interesting thing about that story was when I moved in to my present home, a lady was sitting in the chair in my living room – Eileen – and she was telling me all about her troubles. Then she said that she was in the South Hants hospital. I asked when. She was in there when I was and on the day the hospital was evacuated as well. She was a Wren and we were both evacuated. We went on a fleet of single-decker buses as ambulances. It took us something like fifteen hours to get from Southampton to Basingstoke. They cleared the mental hospital in Park Pruett. All the patients from the South Hants and from St Thomas's in London went into Park Pruett hospital. Eileen was on the bus. I was talking about what happened on my bus. We had a very, very overweight lady on my bus and she screamed all the way there – she thought she was going to fall off the bench. You know how wide a bus seat is, well there was a series of two, three tier ledges that we had to be put on to, to sleep on, to travel on, one on each side of the bus. There was just enough room down the middle for the nurses to attend to people. The fat lady had had appendicitis so she happened to be in the hospital. She was evacuated, too.

Joan Shergold

My father, Ben Parker, was the only survivor in an air raid. His mother was killed and four or five brothers and sisters were also killed. He was ten years old and they dug him out. He spent months in hospital. He was in Northam. The Germans were after the spitfire factory so they blitzed the whole bottom of town one night. That whole area resembled the Inner Avenue area – rows of terraced houses. He was the only survivor. He wrote a letter to his father from his hospital bed. He died in 1998. He always said he remembered looking up and there was a crack up through the ground. He remembered being buried but he said what might have kept him alive was the crack and the air line coming down. He was buried for some hours. His father dug him out. He dug them all out – his wife and four or five of his children, and my father. I always remember my grandfather, Ben. He had white hair. He had very thick, almost like Afro hair, and it was totally white and I said, 'Why do you have such white hair?' and he said he literally went white overnight. If you think about it four or five people would all have had

Little Ben Parker, dirty knees and all, in happy days before the Southampton blitz. (Courtesy of Geoff Parker)

Ben Parker was ten when he wrote this sad letter to his father. He lost his mother and all his siblings when the air raid shelter they were in was hit. His father dug them all out. (Courtesy of Geoff Parker)

Ben Parker, on the right, with relatives. (Courtesy of Geoff Parker)

The street party on the green to celebrate VE-Day. Leah Keable is far right, holding a platter of food. (Courtesy of Eleanor van der Hoest)

VE-Day celebration at Heath Road Junior School. (Courtesy of Joan Shergold)

children and they would have had children who are not here. That is why I do not have much family.

Geoff Parker

VE-Day Celebrations

There's a green outside my grandparents' house in Cypress Avenue and that green used to be fenced off so you couldn't go and play football on it. Apparently, when they held VE-Day celebrations they had special permission to use the green to have a street party.

Eleanor van der Hoest

There was a VE Day party at Heath Road Junior School in the front playground. I was seventeen. The party was for the children. I was allowed to go but not to eat anything. As I walked around to the party a lady with two babies in a pram was walking along and we walked along together. She knew my mother.

'Oh Joan, my goodness me, look at you, what are you going to do now the war is finished? What have you got in mind?'

'One thing I am looking forward to is a banana, a real banana,' I said. She reached down into her pram and came out with a banana.

'Don't wait any longer, Joan,' she said, 'have this one.'

I said, 'But it's the children's.'

'No,' she said, 'they can have a banana anytime. Have this one.'

I ate that banana on the way to the party and, for me, that symbolised VE-Day.

Joan Shergold

Other titles published by The History Press

Haunted Southampton
PENNY LEGG

Uncover the darkest secrets of Southampton's past with this collection of stories of the ghostly apparitions that have haunted residents of the city for centuries. From the Roman soldiers who pervade Bitterne Manor to the Grey Lady at the Royal Victoria Country Park, the site of a former military hospital, the city is host to spirits not yet departed. Southampton is 'alive' with ghosts and, for those who dare, their stories can be discovered in this chilling book.

978 0 7524 5519 8

Growing up in Wartime Southampton
Someone Else's Trousers
JAMES MARSH

James Marsh was born during the first year of the Second World War and many of his infant years were spent in air-raid shelters outside his home. The gritty determination, community spirit and, above all, the humour with which the local community faced the difficulties of war, have stayed with James throughout his life. This book reveals how growing up in the post-war years was both a challenge and a lot of fun.

978 0 7524 5840 3

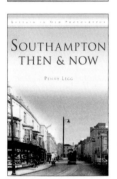

Southampton Then & Now
PENNY LEGG

The major port city of Southampton has a rich heritage, which is uniquely reflected in this fascinating new compilation. Contrasting a rare selection of archive images with full-colour modern photographs, this book reveals the ever-changing faces and buildings of Southampton. Covering local landmarks, pubs and hotels, churches, parks, transport, work and leisure, this is a wide-ranging look at the city's colourful history.

978 0 7524 5693 5

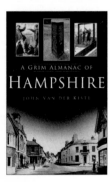

A Grim Almanac of Hampshire
JOHN VAN DER KISTE

A Grim Almanac of Hampshire is a day-by-day catalogue of 366 ghastly tales from the county's past, full of dreadful deeds, macabre deaths, grisly accidents and strange occurrences. Among the gruesome tales included here are the delivery of a foul-smelling basket to a servant in Winchester in 1825, which on investigation was found to contain the body of a stillborn baby, and the double murder of Lydia and Norma Leakey in the New Forest in 1956. All these, plus tales of executions, disasters, suicides, explosions, and accidents by land, sea and air, and much more, are here.

978 0 7524 5489 4

Visit our website and discover thousands of other History Press books.

www.thehistorypress.co.uk

The Histo Press